Paralegal

Advance Praise for *Paralegal*

"Must reading for those contemplating a career move in this direction or those in the profession looking to move up."
—Patricia Wirth
Executive Director
National Capital Area Paralegal
Association

"A great resource for anyone who aspires to the paralegal profession . . . informative, thorough, and well researched."
—Therese A. Cannon
Dean, School of Paralegal Studies
University of West Los Angeles

"Barbara Bernardo has taken the mystery out of the paralegal profession . . . [she] offers a wealth of much-needed insight into the world of paralegals."
—Richard A. Kowall
Director, Paralegal Studies Program
University of San Francisco

"I highly recommend Paralegal *for anyone thinking about entering this booming profession."*
—Patricia Duran
Past President
San Francisco Association of Legal
Assistants

Paralegal

An Insider's Guide to the Fastest-Growing Occupation of the 1990s

Barbara Bernardo

Peterson's Guides

Princeton, New Jersey

Library of Congress Cataloging-in-Publication Data
Bernardo, Barbara, 1952–
    Paralegal : an insider's guide to the fastest-growing
occupation of the 1990s / Barbara Bernardo.
        p.   cm.
    Includes bibliographical references.
    ISBN 0-87866-974-4
    1. Legal assistants—Vocational guidance—United States.
I. Title.
KF320.L4B473   1990
340'.023'73—dc20
                                                90-37586
                                                CIP

Composition and design by Peterson's Guides

Cover design by Carol Larisch-Parise

Printed in the United States of America

10 9 8 7 6 5 4 3 2 1

To my husband, David, whose love and support know no bounds.

Contents

(continued)

Preface

In 1987, the U.S. Department of Labor predicted that the paralegal field would be the fastest-growing occupation of the 1990s. As a result, in the past few years, interest in the field has grown tremendously. However, there are still many misconceptions about paralegals and what they do. Although I have been working as a paralegal since 1979, most people that I know still don't understand what I do for a living. Questions range from "You're like a legal secretary, right?" to "I have a legal problem. Can you help me?" This book is an effort to clear up some of those misconceptions. I discovered that most books about the field were either handbooks or manuals for working paralegals or career books written in the early 1980s by attorneys, headhunters, and educators who had only secondhand knowledge of paralegals. I felt the time was right for a career book written by a paralegal.

Unlike people today who choose the paralegal field by design, I discovered it quite by accident in the late 1970s when I needed extra income to supplement my work as a dancer and choreographer. It took me only a short while to realize that the paralegal profession had great career potential. As I gained experience, I was intrigued by the notion that I was doing legal tasks that people assumed were far too difficult for anyone other than an attorney. I learned that not all legal work is the same. That is, there are varying degrees of complexity in legal tasks, many of which can be performed by nonlawyers at a much lower cost to clients. More important, when I discovered that most legal work required 10 percent strategy and 90 percent common sense, the mystique surrounding law and lawyers disappeared.

Today, I'm more convinced than ever that the paralegal field is important not only as an interesting career but as a viable answer to pent-up consumer demand for affordable legal services. I believe there's room in our legal system for different levels of professionals to offer varying degrees of legal expertise directly to the public. Such a hierarchy already exists in the area of income tax preparation—anyone from a tax attorney to the person next door can legally prepare an income tax form.

While everyone may not agree with the idea of allowing nonlawyers to offer services to the public, the concept is currently being explored by the state bar of California. In August 1989, the bar voted on a resolution to study the idea of legal technicians offering basic legal services to the public. The issue is not resolved. If California does allow legal technicians to, in effect, "practice law," it will be an unprecedented decision not only for consumers but for the paralegal field as well.

It appears as if the paralegal profession has taken the advice of Jean-Jacques Rousseau, who so brilliantly stated:

> *Take the course opposite to custom and you will almost always do well.*

Barbara Bernardo

Acknowledgments

I would like to express my sincere thanks to those individuals whose contributions, both directly and indirectly, made this book possible: Kathy Allen, Larry Ausink, Therese Cannon, Chyllene Cattie, Julie Champion, Doris Childs, Patricia O. Curtis, Teri L. Dellinger-Schroeder, Patricia Duran, Lucy Ebersohl, Joan Elliott, Chere B. Estrin, Linda Harrington, E. Earl Hauss, Lyla Hines, Mary Hitt, Royanne Hollins, Beverlee Johnson, Karen B. Judd, Richard A. Kowall, Jill Martin, Carolyn McKown, Jolene Miller, Loretta Nesbitt, John F. O'Flaherty, Susan Peifer, Lynn Pelletier, Diane Remick, Laurie Roselle, Arnold H. Rosenberg, Linda E. Roye, Peggy Ruse, Jon Sargent, Mary Beth Schultz, Denise Templeton, Laura Thomas, Ingrid Tronsrue, Steve Wagner, Patricia A. Wirth, and Paul Zavalney.

I would also like to thank the following organizations for graciously providing the salary surveys and other valuable information: American Bar Association, Dallas Association of Legal Assistants, Georgia Association of Legal Assistants, Kansas City Association of Legal Assistants, Los Angeles Paralegal Association, Minnesota Association of Legal Assistants, National Association of Legal Assistants, National Capital Area Paralegal Association, National Federation of Paralegal Associations, Rocky Mountain Legal Assistants Association, St. Louis Association of Legal Assistants, San Francisco Association of Legal Assistants, the Philadelphia Institute, and the Washington Legal Assistants Association 1988 Professional Development Committee.

Finally, I would like to thank Peterson's Guides; its editorial director James Gish for believing in this project from beginning to end; and my editors, Joy Mastroberardino and Larry Wexler, and proofreader Paula Williams for helping to pull the manuscript together for publication.

Introduction

The concept of the paraprofessional is not new. The fields of dentistry and medicine have been using paraprofessionals—dental hygienists and nurses—for years. Yet the legal profession discovered the benefits of paralegals only two decades ago. Paralegals are part of an innovative, nontraditional, evolving field that is helping to change the practice of law.

This book is for recent high school or college graduates; people looking for a new career, reentering the work force, or contemplating law or business school; those who want to work in the legal industry without going to law school; and students who are attending paralegal training programs. (Attorneys who are contemplating using paralegals in their law practice will find it useful, too.) It will help you to decide whether a paralegal career is right for you by providing an inside, personal look at the fastest-growing occupation of the 1990s and answers to the following questions:

- What is a paralegal?
- What's the difference between a paralegal and a lawyer?
- Where do paralegals work?
- How much do paralegals earn?
- What education, training, and skills are needed to become a paralegal?
- How do you find your first paralegal job?
- What advancement opportunities are available?
- What does the future hold for the profession?

The book also explains how and why the paralegal field evolved, the trends in the legal industry that affect the profession, how computers affect on-the-job tasks and career opportunities, and the issues that face paralegals.

This is an excellent time to be considering a career as a paralegal. It's a flexible profession: it can be a career in itself, a stepping-stone to other careers, or a foundation for law or business school. It's dynamic: it's on the cutting edge of a changing industry. And it's challenging: the inroads into our legal system made by paralegals today will affect legal services well into the twenty-first century.

Chapter

Paralegal: The New Frontier

I do not believe you can do today's job with yesterday's methods and be in business tomorrow.

Nelson Jackson

The profession of law is centuries old, and until just a few years ago, "yesterday's methods" worked just fine. Not anymore. The legal profession is undergoing dramatic changes, not the least of which is the evolution of a new profession of nonlawyers called legal assistants or paralegals. (The terms legal assistant and paralegal are interchangeable.) This exciting and innovative profession is revolutionizing the practice of law.

While the paralegal field has been in existence for almost twenty years, until recently few people had ever heard of it. The U.S. Department of Labor has changed all that. Upon reviewing over 500 occupations for its 1987 and 1989 employment surveys, the Department of Labor projected the paralegal profession to be the fastest-growing occupation of all. This status may be attributed to the increased consumer demand for affordable legal services, the overburdened court system, and the increased use of paralegals by attorneys. In addition, the 1988 *Jobs Rated Almanac*, published by American Reference, Inc., rated paralegal tenth best in its study of the 250 best and worst jobs, using salary, work environment, employment outlook, job security, stress, and physical demands as the criteria.

Despite this publicity, many people still don't know what a paralegal is or does. Even fewer know how and why the field has become the fast growth profession of the decade. This chapter will introduce you to the profession and help clear away some of the

3

misconceptions about it and, in so doing, will be a starting point for your evaluation of this career opportunity.

What Is a Paralegal?

Simply put, paralegals are nonlawyers who perform legal tasks that were once done only by lawyers. The rationale for their existence is that legal matters can be broken down into small components and tasks that can be delegated to nonlawyers working under supervision. If this concept doesn't seem especially new or revolutionary, that's because it isn't. Industry adapted it when it changed from piecemeal to assembly line production. Henry Ford used it to build cars, believing that while one individual might be incapable of building an entire car, he or she was capable of assembling one or two of its components. In so doing, the individual could become an expert at a particular task. The point is, whether the job is building a car or tackling a legal problem, a task can be broken down into various parts that can be performed by many different people.

Termed division of labor, it was this process of dividing work among individuals that helped Ford and others mass produce goods, maintain relatively high quality standards, and lower the price of products to levels the general public could afford. Similarly, the goal of dividing work between lawyers and paralegals is to make it possible to deliver high-quality and affordable legal services to an ever-increasing number of clients.

The idea that paralegals can perform tasks done by lawyers intrigues me. Before I became a paralegal, I felt intimidated by lawyers, as most people do. I thought since lawyers charge so much money and use Latin words, what they do has to be incomprehensible to an ordinary person.

But that's just not true. After my first year, I began to experience a process that I fondly call the demystification of the law. I knew it was completed one day when I read a fifty-page legal document and understood what it said.

Formal Definitions

But back to the original question: What is a paralegal? What follows are three formal definitions that have been developed over the past several years by lawyers and paralegals. Note that the significant difference between these definitions is the phrase "under the supervision of an attorney." The majority of paralegals work directly under the supervision of an attorney, while a small minority provide basic legal services directly to the public, as will be discussed further in Chapter 10.

The American Bar Association (ABA) defines paralegals as:

> *persons who, although not members of the legal profession, are qualified through education, training or work experience, are employed or retained by a lawyer, law office, governmental agency, or other entity in a capacity or function which involves the performance, under the direction and supervision of an attorney, of specifically-delegated substantive legal work, which work, for the most part, requires a sufficient knowledge of legal concepts, such that, absent that legal assistant, the attorney would perform the task.*

Believe it or not, that's one sentence. But lawyers, as you may already know, are fond of using long sentences with many commas. This language is commonly referred to as legalese. As I said, after a year or two as a paralegal you won't be intimidated by it.

In 1984, the National Association of Legal Assistants (NALA) developed the following definition.

> *Legal Assistants* are a distinguishable group of persons who assist attorneys in the delivery of legal services. Through formal education, training, and experience, legal assistants have knowledge and expertise regarding the legal system and substantive and procedural law which qualify them to do work of a legal nature under the supervision of an attorney.*Within this occupational category, some individuals are known as paralegals.*

The National Federation of Paralegal Associations (NFPA) prepared the following definition in 1987.

> *A paralegal/legal assistant is a person qualified through education, training, or work experience to perform substantive legal work that requires knowledge of legal concepts and is customarily, but not exclusively, performed by a lawyer.*

According to these definitions, a paralegal is an individual who, because of education, training, or work experience, performs various legal tasks under the supervision of an attorney. But this summary still doesn't reveal what paralegals actually do. As such, the definition has to be refined to take into account the type of employer (law firm, corporation, or government agency), the size of the employer, the legal specialty area (litigation, corporate, real estate, probate, etc.), the types of cases handled, the types of clients, the employer's attitude toward paralegals, and the specific skills, education, and background the paralegal brings to the job. The role of every paralegal is defined by these factors.

In addition, they are important to consider when looking for a paralegal position. As you'll see from reading other chapters in this book, they can make the difference between a good job and a great one.

Another problem encountered when trying to define what a paralegal is is the term paralegal itself. For instance, a paralegal who works in the area of estate planning in a small firm has a totally different set of responsibilities than a paralegal who works in employee benefits in a corporation. While each holds the title paralegal, the duties performed are so different that it's impossible to compare the jobs or their salary levels. (This is discussed at length in Chapter 5.)

How Do Paralegals and Lawyers Differ?

Another way to answer the question "What is a paralegal?" is to look at what paralegals can't do and at the division of labor between them and lawyers.

Paralegals Cannot Practice Law

First, let's look at what paralegals can't do. In a nutshell, paralegals aren't permitted to practice law. But what does that mean? Simply put, paralegals *cannot* give legal advice, set legal fees, or represent clients in court—these are tasks only attorneys can do. Everything else is pretty much fair game.

Strategists and Technicians

When I first became a paralegal, the paralegal coordinator asked me to prepare a job description of my duties and responsibilities. I had trouble distinguishing between what I did and what first- and second-year associates did. At times, it seemed as if we were doing the same things. A fellow paralegal who had been at the firm for several years pointed out the difference to me: the attorney knows what to do and the paralegal knows how to do it. To put it another way, the lawyer is the strategist, and the paralegal, who implements the strategy, is the technician. In theory, at least, that's how it's supposed to work.

To illustrate this concept, let's say you start your own company. While you may know that it could be formed as a corporation, partnership, or sole proprietorship, you don't have the legal expertise to decide which would be best for your situation. So you enlist the services of a lawyer, who sits down with you, asks some basic questions, and decides that your company should be formed as a corporation.

The lawyer used his or her knowledge of the legal principles of corporations (learned in law school) to make this decision. The lawyer has decided what to do—and planned the strategy. A paralegal wouldn't and shouldn't make that kind of strategic decision, which is, essentially, practicing law. A paralegal who does would be engaged in the *unauthorized* practice of law.

Let's carry the example one step further. If your company is to be incorporated, certain paperwork must be prepared. But by whom? A sharp attorney will enlist the services of a paralegal to draft the incorporation documents. (If not, be prepared for an unnecessarily high bill.) The paralegal, as technician, knows how to implement the attorney's strategic plan.

I can't emphasize enough that the parameters of what paralegals can and can't do are in part dictated by the attitudes of lawyers toward them. Some lawyers know how to use paralegals; others don't. This is important to consider when you're looking for a job.

The Value of the Difference Between Lawyer and Paralegal

Interestingly, the roles played by the lawyer and paralegal in the preceding example underscore why paralegal services are increasingly valued by clients.

Think about it. Suppose in the incorporation case the lawyer informs the client that it will take approximately 5 hours to prepare the documents. Say the attorney charges $200 per hour and the hourly rate for paralegals is $50. Simple arithmetic indicates that it would be more economical for a paralegal to help draft the incorporation papers. Of course, the lawyer would still need to review the work, but that would only take an hour. If a paralegal is used, the client would pay $50/hour × 5 hours ($250) plus $200/hour × 1 hour ($200) for the attorney, for a grand total of $450. Compare that to the $1,000 that would have been charged if the lawyer had done all the work! You can see how paralegals help reduce legal fees.

But how does an attorney benefit from using a paralegal? First, rather than devote time to fairly routine legal tasks, the attorney can spend more time making strategic decisions that require the application of legal training and expertise. Second, lower fees tend to make clients happy—and satisfied customers are good for any business. Third, if lawyers can delegate routine work to paralegals, it is likely that the firm will be able to handle a greater volume of work. Fourth, firms need not put as many highly paid associate attorneys on staff to do routine legal tasks, which can mean a considerable savings in labor costs and overhead. The bottom line is that because using paralegals makes legal services more affordable, clients and law firms both gain.

Before looking at the differences between paralegals and other legal personnel, I should mention the most basic distinction between lawyers and paralegals. That is, attorneys have the ultimate responsibility for all of the work done on a case. That's why they're paid more.

I found this to be one of the benefits of a paralegal career. I was free to pursue other interests and I never lost a single night's sleep worrying about a case. I'm sure the same can't be said for some of the attorneys I worked for. Of course, this doesn't mean that if you become a paralegal you should do less than your best possible work. It all boils down to how much responsibility you want out of a job and a career.

Other Legal Personnel

As a paralegal, you'll encounter other types of legal personnel—particularly if you work in a law firm. If the lawyer is the strategist and the paralegal is the technician, what are the functions of the legal secretary, law clerk, and legal administrator?

Generally speaking, the legal secretary types correspondence and legal documents, answers the telephone, maintains files, makes appointments for the attorney, keeps the attorney's calendar, files papers with the court, and maintains time sheets.

The law clerk is a law school student usually hired for the summer to perform legal research, draft legal documents, attend hearings with attorneys, and interview clients. (A paralegal's duties closely resemble those of a law clerk. The difference is that the clerk is given more substantive legal research and less "grunt" work, so to speak.)

Finally, the legal administrator is involved in administrative functions of the office, such as preparing budgets; overseeing payroll and accounting for the firm; hiring, firing, and other personnel functions; negotiating with vendors; handling matters related to the leasing of law office space; assessing equipment needs and purchasing equipment (such as computer systems); and managing the office.

It's important to understand that the responsibilities and duties of each of these positions may overlap those of paralegals, depending on the size of the law firm, the attitude of the firm toward each position, and the size of the firm's budget. For instance, in a small law firm with a limited budget, the paralegal may be required to perform some of the functions of a legal administrator and/or a legal secretary.

Evolution of the Profession

As I said earlier, while the paralegal field is barely twenty years old, it has undergone extensive, even dynamic, changes. It has witnessed its own birth, infancy, and childhood; adolescence and the growing pains that come with it; and, as it enters its third decade, early adulthood and maturity.

It should come as no surprise that the profession had its beginnings in the 1960s. It's easy to see how a concept as innovative as paraprofessionals for the practice of law had its roots in a decade whose buzzword was change. However, it's worth noting that even before this development, many legal secretaries performed tasks that are now performed by paralegals. The role of legal secretaries in the development of the profession can't be underestimated; they were the forerunners of the modern-day paralegal.

The 1960s and Early 1970s: Birth and Childhood

During the 1960s and early 1970s, our society experienced many social, demographic, technological, and economic changes that have had a lasting impact on our legal system. Some of these developments include:

- Changes in basic social attitudes toward work, sex, the status and role of women, the family unit, minorities, and equal oppportunity;
- Rising expectations of fairness and justice due to changes in social attitudes toward equality;
- Changes in national demographics, including the size and age of the population, the birthrate, migration patterns, and family size and structure;
- Greater concentration of people in urban areas leading to increased crime and urban decay;
- Increases in the number of government regulations and laws due to growing public concerns about worker safety, environmental pollution, and health care;
- Advances in technology and communications resulting in a shift from a production- to a service-oriented economy; and
- Heightened consumer consciousness leading to greater

awareness of consumer rights and a consumer protection movement.

For the legal profession, these changes translated into a greater demand for legal services, an increase in the number and complexity of laws, rising expectations of justice, and an overburdened court system. The legal industry responded in various ways, most notably by creating a new professional niche within itself—the legal paraprofessional.

From legal secretary to paraprofessional. The paralegals we know today didn't just appear out of the blue in the late 1960s and early 1970s. The profession evolved gradually. In fact, before the term paralegal was even used, individuals who worked in private law firms and federal government agencies had been performing paralegal-type functions.

Eventually, as more demands were placed upon the legal system, it became clear that the lawyer/legal secretary team at many law firms could no longer handle the work load. As a result, many legal secretaries found themselves performing paralegal-type functions in addition to their secretarial tasks. For instance, it was common for a legal secretary to draft as well as type legal documents. As legal secretaries handled more paraprofessional tasks and fewer clerical ones, the new profession was born.

At the same time, a change in social attitude led to an increase in the number of federal programs serving the poor and elderly. Social workers employed in food stamp, public housing, Medicare, and Social Security programs began to perform more and more paralegal-type tasks as part of their job. Thus, by the late 1960s, the federal government was already using many individuals in a paralegal capacity.

Formal recognition of the profession. The next phase in the development of the paralegal field was marked by formal recognition of its existence. This recognition came on many fronts—from the ABA, the federal government, educational institutions, and paralegals themselves.

The first step toward formal recognition occurred in 1968 when the ABA established its Special Committee on Lay Assistants for Lawyers. Its purpose was twofold: (1) to study how lawyers could effectively use nonlawyers and (2) to determine educational requirements and standards for paralegal education. Interestingly, the committee looked at other professions, such as medicine, dentistry, and architecture, that had been using paraprofessionals for years and concluded that the legal industry could profit from the use of paraprofessionals. As it turns out, history proved the committee right.

The committee has since changed its name to the Standing Committee on Legal Assistants and continues to work with national paralegal associations toward the development of standards for paralegal education. As you'll read in Chapter 6, some form of paralegal training—whether a paralegal certificate or an associate or bachelor's degree in paralegal studies—is becoming increasingly important for people planning to enter the field. Many employers require that prospective paralegal employees be graduates of ABA-approved programs.

Around the time the ABA committee was created, the federal government recognized the beneficial role of legal paraprofessionals. In 1972, the National Paralegal Institute was established within the federal government's Office of Legal Services. Three years later, the institute began training paralegals and other individuals in the delivery of legal services to the poor and elderly.

Meanwhile, in 1974, President Richard M. Nixon signed into law a bill that set up the Legal Services Corporation, an organization intended to oversee a nationwide legal service program. The corporation used paralegals to help the poor and elderly in civil matters, such as landlord-tenant disputes, job discrimination cases, and divorces.

Another important development toward recognition came with the emergence and growth of paralegal educational institutions. Responding to the increased need for trained paralegals, a handful of schools began to offer courses in the early 1970s that led to paralegal certification. Perhaps the most famous is the Philadelphia Institute (formerly the Philadelphia Institute for Paralegal Training). Before these schools were established, on-the-job training and/or a promotion from legal secretary were the only ways to enter the field. Recognizing the growing popularity of paralegal training programs, in 1972 the ABA developed standards for accrediting formal education programs. Today there are over 500 educational institutions that offer paralegal training programs. Of them, only 130 or so are ABA approved.

The last major development toward formal recognition was spearheaded by paralegals themselves: the formation of two major professional associations. In the early 1970s, they formed the National Federation of Paralegal Associations and the National Association of Legal Assistants to further the development of the profession and protect and promote the interests of their member-ships. (As Chapter 8 suggests, joining a paralegal association is an excellent way to obtain information about the paralegal profession and develop useful contacts for paralegal employment.)

Mid-1970s to Mid-1980s: Adolescence

After receiving formal recognition, the profession experienced a difficult phase in its development. As with all adolescents, it expe-rienced growing pains, confusion, self-doubt, and an identity cri-sis. No one really knew what to do with paralegals. Were they lawyers or secretaries, or something in-between?

Since the field was relatively new, many lawyers were reluctant to delegate complex legal tasks to paralegals. As such, from the mid-1970s to the mid-1980s, the work of many paralegals was highly clerical—organizing, indexing, sorting, photocopying, and the like. Simply put, paralegals were being underutilized.

However, as lawyers learned to use them in more sophisticated ways, paralegals began to take on greater responsibilities. By the late 1980s, a pool of experienced paralegals had developed. These individuals paved the way for today's paralegals.

Late 1980s and Beyond: Young Adulthood

The awkwardness of adolescence has finally given way to a maturity that is sure to characterize the field in the next decade. Paralegals are now accepted as a fact of life in the legal profession. They are handling more sophisticated tasks as the lines between themselves and attorneys blur.

This is truly an exciting time to be considering a paralegal career. More than ever before, paralegals are taking the direction of the profession into their own hands. As Laurie Roselle, parale-gal coordinator at Rogers & Wells in New York City, so aptly states, "My attitude is 'Let me define the parameters of what I can do, not people who think they know what a paralegal is and does.' I enjoy what I'm doing as a paralegal and I believe very strongly that the whole reason for the creation of the paralegal profession is to be able to deliver quality legal services at a lower cost than an attor-ney."

Perhaps the most striking example of the maturing of the para-legal profession comes from the California State Bar Association. In August 1989, it voted to establish a panel to study the idea of allowing nonlawyers called legal technicians to provide routine legal services directly to the public. This is an unprecedented move on the part of a state bar association. If it's approved, it will signify a turning point for the profession, since it would mean paralegals could offer services without the supervision of attorneys.

In spite of that optimistic possibility, you should be aware that even today there are lawyers who haven't recognized the benefits of using paralegals. Within the same law firm, some lawyers are resistant to using paralegals while others can't live without them. This is something else to keep in mind when you look for a paralegal job: don't be surprised if you run into lawyers who still believe paralegals are nothing more than glorified clerical workers.

Developments in the Legal Industry That Affect Paralegals

There have been substantial changes in the legal profession in the past decade that have directly benefited the paralegal field. Certain trends and developments continue to move the field in a positive direction. The ten developments that follow are bound to affect you in one way or another if you choose to pursue a paralegal career in the 1990s.

Growth of the Legal Services Industry

The baby boom of the late 1940s and 1950s led to a major growth spurt in the population of post–World War II America. In the 1960s and 1970s, the baby boomers made their way into schools and colleges and became highly conscious of ways in which the legal system could be used to correct perceived grievances in society.

Coupled with increased aspirations for justice and equality by other groups in our society, these factors are often cited as key to the growing demand for legal services. In fact, between 1980 and 1988, the amount spent on legal services nearly tripled, from $26-billion to $73-billion.

Greater demand for services has meant more lawsuits. Between 1977 and 1987, civil cases in federal district courts increased 83 percent, from 130,600 to 239,000 cases per year. The legal industry responded to this increased work load by employing more workers, including paralegals. From 1977 to 1987, the head count in law firms more than doubled, from 392,000 to 808,000. Between 1980 and 1988, the number of paralegals increased 130 percent, from 36,000 to approximately 83,000. (Since the U.S. Department of Labor didn't begin until 1980 to gather information about those working as paralegals, it's difficult to provide accurate statistics prior to that time.)

Increased Demand for Affordable Legal Services

"Affordability" is the buzzword in the legal industry today. People across the country are fed up with the high price of lawyers and are demanding high-quality services at reasonable prices. Many large law firms charge as much as $350 to $400 per hour for the services of their senior partners. Consequently, virtually everyone from the little guy to the multinational corporation now scrutinizes legal bills. Gone are the days when a typical invoice might state, "For legal services rendered—$50,000"—no questions asked! Times have changed.

The demand for affordable legal services means that paralegals can play a pivotal role in the future delivery of those services. Lawyers can no longer ignore the benefits of using them. As I pointed out earlier, paralegals are cost-effective for the client and the firm.

Oversupply of Lawyers

How many times have you heard someone complain that there are just too many lawyers? From 1970 to 1988, the number of lawyers has grown 100 percent, from 350,000 to 700,000. Quite a jump, considering that it's totally out of proportion to the growth of the general population, which increased by 19 percent over the same period.

The proven cost-effectiveness of paralegals raises the question of whether we need more lawyers or more paralegals. The answer is tricky. We actually need both. But in what proportion? The law of supply and demand would seem to be on the side of the paralegal. Today, for reasons related primarily to productivity and cost savings, a law firm is more apt to hire two experienced paralegals and one associate rather than three associates as they might have in the past. (That's another reason the employment outlook for paralegals in the 1990s is so favorable.)

Increased Competition

Interestingly, as the number of lawyers increased, competition within the legal industry increased as well. Adding to this pressure is the growing sophistication of clients who shop around for the lowest possible legal fees. All of this has forced law firms to reexamine the way they do business.

The responses have varied and include, of course, the use of paralegals to help reduce client bills. (I have yet to meet a client who objects to a lower bill.)

Advertising and Marketing

Another response to increased competition is the use of advertising and marketing to attract clients. While these techniques have been used for many years by most businesses, the courts relaxed the rules governing advertising by lawyers only within the last decade. The upshot is that firms are beginning to make use of marketing and public relations professionals. This may be good news for paralegals who want to use their career as a stepping-stone to a job in public relations or marketing, as you will see in Chapter 9.

Greater Specialization

In recent years, there has been a trend toward greater specialization within the law. As with medicine, the days of the general practitioner are gone. There is just too much information for any one person to know. Thus, lawyers are becoming experts in specific areas of law, such as taxation, securities, bankruptcy, immigration, and so forth, and boutique law firms that offer expertise in a particular specialty area are emerging.

What does this mean for the paralegal? Everything! As you'll see in Chapter 8, the trend toward specialization is an important key to higher salary and greater paralegal job satisfaction.

Computers and Technology

The legal profession has been slower than most others in accepting the benefits of computers. Until recently, lawyers couldn't figure out how to use computers for anything other than billing purposes. Today, however, the applications for computers in law range from litigation support systems and legal research to preparing wills and incorporations. (There are software programs in development that even mimic how a lawyer thinks and analyzes legal problems.)

For paralegals, the trend toward the increased use of computers and technology is a gold mine! Computer-literate paralegals tend to enjoy greater job satisfaction, increased compensation, and more avenues for career advancement, as you'll read in Chapter 7. I can't emphasize enough how important it will be in the future for paralegals to become computer literate.

Alternative Methods of Dispute Resolution

An overburdened judicial system and expensive litigation proceedings have resulted in the use of less formal methods of resolving disputes. One such is arbitration. In it, disputing parties mutually agree to settle the matter by employing a disinterested party, known as an arbitrator, to make a decision that will be binding for them. Another is mediation. It's a less formal, nonbinding method of dispute resolution. The most familiar use of arbitrators and mediators is in the areas of labor disputes and sports negotiations.

The use of paralegals in labor law is increasing. Paralegals not only are assisting lawyers in traditional ways but are using this experience to advance into careers as arbitrators and mediators.

Self-Help Law

Among the more controversial developments is the notion of self-help law. In 1971, Ralph Warner and Charles Sherman pioneered the self-help law movement by cofounding Nolo Press in Berkeley, California, and establishing the WAVE Project. Nolo Press publishes self-help law practice books such as *How to Do Your Own Divorce* and *How to Form Your Own Corporation*. The WAVE Project was the country's first self-help law center at which nonlawyers specialize in preparing divorce forms at significantly lower rates than those charged by attorneys. The concept that guides the movement is that the average person can use self-help publications to draft legal documents that lawyers then need only review, which helps the user save on form preparation, consulting, and other such attorney fees.

Not surprisingly, not everyone in the legal profession is pleased with this concept. Some lawyers believe that filling out the forms needed to prepare one's own divorce or incorporation dangerously walks the line of unauthorized practice of law.

Beyond the WAVE Project, there are paralegals who, with do-it-yourself publications like those from Nolo Press, have started their own paralegal businesses and offer legal services directly to the general public. These independent paralegals have come under a great deal of criticism from the legal profession in general and from some paralegals. The concern is that they may be engaged in the unauthorized practice of law.

Responding to this criticism, the proponents of self-help law ask whether the lawyers are unselfishly concerned with protecting the general public against the unauthorized practice of law or more concerned about possible competition from nonlawyers. This controversial issue is discussed in Chapter 10.

More Effective Use of Paralegals

Last, but certainly not least, is the trend toward hiring more paralegals and using them more effectively. Lawyers are beginning to realize that paralegals can do much more than index and organize documents and are trusting them to perform more of the tasks that they once did themselves.

These are the trends and developments that are shaping and defining the paralegal profession. All will have some bearing on the role and responsibilities of those who enter the field in the 1990s.

Now that you have a better understanding of what a paralegal is, you can begin to decide whether this career is for you. Of course, you'll need information about the specific tasks and responsibilities of paralegals before you can make a full evaluation. But before you look at those, it's important to consider where paralegals work. The workplace helps determine the work environment and, to some degree, the specific duties of paralegals. The next chapter examines this matter.

Chapter

Where Do Paralegals Work?

Nothing is really work unless you would rather be doing something else.

Chub De Wolfe

My first position in law was in 1979 in a small law firm in Hartford, Connecticut. On my second day on the job, one of the attorneys took me aside and said, "I just want you to know that lawyers are a strange breed that takes some getting used to." At the time, I had no idea what he was talking about, since the only contact I had had with attorneys up until then had to do with a relative's will. But now I can unequivocally say that he was right—they do take some getting used to and so does working in a law firm.

For some people, the thought of visiting a law firm, much less working in one, can be quite intimidating. Just looking at all those law books can make them nervous! On the other hand, there are some who find the level of professionalism and intensity at a law firm quite stimulating and challenging. But, while law firms may be the largest employer of paralegals, they certainly aren't the only employer. Others include corporations; banks; insurance companies; federal, state, and local government agencies; nonprofit corporations; legal aid organizations; and paralegal service companies. As discussed below, there are significant differences between working in these organizations, in terms of assignments, salary, benefits, advancement possibilities, and job satisfaction.

Law Firms

In 1985, there were over 42,300 law firms in the United States. Since the majority of paralegals—approximately 80 percent—

work in them, that's where this discussion begins. Law firms come in all shapes and sizes and range from sole practitioners to megafirms with over 900 lawyers. This was not always the case. In an article that appeared in a law journal in 1902, the author made reference to " . . . the Giant Law Firms of five to as many as eight Lawyers." How times have changed.

In the past decade, law firms have undergone many transformations. For instance, in 1978, the average law firm had approximately 100 lawyers. By 1987, that increased to 200. Also, many firms have opened branch offices abroad in response to the globalization of our economy. With growth in firm size comes growth in revenues. In 1987, 21 of the top 100 law firms in the nation had revenues exceeding $100-million—the size of some Fortune 1000 companies! Law is big business.

Some firms have begun to experiment with the concept of in-house consultants. For example, in addition to legal services, some law firms now offer consulting services in the areas of employee benefits, labor relations, health care, environmental and energy issues, real estate development, and so on. These developments in law firm structure—increased size, globalization, and use of in-house nonlawyer specialists—are shaping the environment in which paralegals work.

When you are looking for a job in a law firm, the first question you should ask yourself is whether you want to work in a small, medium, or large firm. Each has its advantages and disadvantages. Understanding the workings of a law firm will help you answer the questions, no matter what size you ultimately choose.

Basically, a firm is either a partnership or a professional corporation. What this means is that a limited number of individuals—the partners or shareholders—own the firm and share in its profits. Think of a pyramid. The partners are at the top and are supported by the larger group of people on the bottom. It's interesting to note that the existing canon of legal ethics prohibits nonlawyers from participating in the ownership or profits of a law firm. The advent of in-house consultants who actively contribute to the firm's profits may cause this to change.

Law Firm Personnel

The goal for most lawyers is to become a partner, and this is usually accomplished by working for approximately seven years as an associate. But as competition between firms increases and profit margins are squeezed, becoming a partner is easier said than done. These days, there are no guarantees that just because an attorney has devoted seven years to a firm he or she will be made a partner.

Associates are hired directly out of law school and from other law firms. Paralegals usually work more with associates than with partners. It's been my experience that associates fresh out of law school generally know less about how to get things done than paralegals with several years' experience. As a result, new associates are sometimes reluctant to ask paralegals for help, but eventually most come to realize that an experienced paralegal is an invaluable asset.

Further down in the law firm hierarchy are the nonlawyer personnel, who include:

- Paralegals and paralegal assistants (sometimes known as case assistants);
- Administrative staff, such as librarians and office managers; and
- Clerical staff, such as secretaries, word processors, messengers, receptionists, and file clerks.

The order of this list is not meant to imply that any one group is more important than another. (You'll find out just how important the file clerk's job is when a file has been misplaced!) As a paralegal you'll interact with these other support staffers daily, though, depending on the size of the firm, some of the positions may not exist. For instance, a small law firm usually doesn't have a librarian or in-house messengers.

Paralegals and legal secretaries. Paralegals generally share a secretary with a partner, one or two associates, or any combination of the two. I would be remiss if I didn't mention the tension that may exist between legal secretaries and paralegals—there are several reasons for it. As an occupation, legal secretary has been around much longer than paralegal. Also, as I mentioned earlier, legal secretaries were in a sense the forerunner of paralegals. I've found that a lawyer generally develops a unique relationship with his or her secretary: each is devoutly loyal to the other. What does this mean for the paralegal? Basically, be good to the secretary. I know it sounds trite, but in reality a secretary can make your life infinitely easier or make it miserable. The bottom line is that the partner, associate, paralegal, and secretary must all work together to deliver the best possible service to the client.

21

Clients

Clients come in many shapes and sizes. They may be individuals, small companies, or multinational corporations and everything in-between. When I worked for a large law firm, the clients I worked for included a large California bank, San Francisco brokerage firms, a multinational oil company, start-up high-tech computer companies, restaurants and wineries, an ice cream manufacturer, a department store, a lily bulb grower, an exporter of Oriental goods, a sugar company, and a mining company.

It's important to understand that the type of work performed by paralegals in law firms is directly related to the firm's clientele. In turn, the clientele is usually determined by the size of the law firm. For instance, most individuals and small companies can't afford the expensive rates charged by large firms. As a result, the majority of the clients of large law firms are corporations. It follows then, that, in a large firm, no matter what legal specialty area the paralegal works in, the assignments are likely to involve the affairs of a corporation.

Large firms are usually organized by specialty groups—litigation, bankruptcy, real estate, probate, securities, and so on. Each group has a supervising partner in charge of it, and the partner has a number of associates working under her or him. At least one paralegal is assigned to each group. As a result, the paralegals as well as the attorneys become specialists in the area. In small firms, paralegals often work in more than one specialty area. As you can see, the size of the firm is an important factor when considering paralegal employment.

Billable Hours

Common to all law firms, no matter what their size, is the notion of billable and nonbillable hours. Clients are charged on an hourly basis for the services performed by the partners, associates, paralegals, and paralegal assistants and, sometimes, for word processing services. Generally, firms don't charge for a secretary's time.

What does this mean for you as a paralegal? It means you must account for most or all of your time each day—your billable and nonbillable hours. Billable hours are those spent on matters that can be charged directly to clients. Nonbillable hours are spent on matters that are not directly related to clients, such as administrative tasks and *pro bono* work. (*Pro bono publico* is Latin for "for the public good or welfare" and means a case taken on for free. These can be the most interesting to work on.) Billable hours are directly related to firm profits. Firms sometimes set a minimum number of billable hours for paralegals, as they do for attorneys.

Law Firm Size

The question now is what size law firm to work in—large, medium, or small? I've worked in all three and can honestly say that each has its pros and cons. The size of a law firm is relative and depends on the number of attorneys it employs and its geographic location. For instance, a medium-sized law firm in New York City may employ 200 lawyers while a firm with the same number of attorneys in a smaller city might be considered large. For simplicity's sake, let's say that large means 100 or more lawyers, medium is 50–99 lawyers, and small is 1–49 lawyers.

Large law firms. Working in a large firm has several advantages. The most obvious is that a large firm has more resources to tap into—an extensive law library, photocopy and word processing centers, and in-house messengers, among other things.

I can recall going from a small firm of 14 attorneys in New York to a large firm of 200-plus attorneys in San Francisco. What struck me first was that I could delegate the more routine tasks to various departments in the large firm. At the small firm, if I wanted three copies of a 100-page document and the secretary was busy, guess who did it? In a large firm I could give it to the photocopy center. This structure allows paralegals to perform more sophisticated tasks and not spend valuable time at the copy machine.

A wonderful development is the advent of case assistants, who assist paralegals on large cases. They do a lot of the document organizaton, indexing, and general clerical work. A case assistant career track in a law firm provides another opportunity for individuals to be promoted to paralegals. Unfortunately, not all law firms use case assistants. As a result, some paralegals spend more of their time on clerical tasks, which can create frustration and dissatisfaction and lead to high turnover rates.

A large firm may also offer a structured paralegal system that might include a paralegal manager, an in-house paralegal training program, paralegal staff meetings, in-house seminars, and in-house advancement opportunities. I found it quite beneficial to have a paralegal supervisor available to act as the liaison between management and me regarding work assignments and salary. In-house training, which includes the use of the law library and computerized legal research systems, is particularly useful to new paralegals without prior job experience. Large firms regularly schedule paralegal staff meetings and seminars on various legal topics, which offer the opportunity to network and get to know your fellow paralegals. (The larger the firm, the more paralegals.) Also, many large firms that wish to retain experienced paralegals have created a senior paralegal job track. This advanced position often includes certain perquisites such as more vacation, parking, a higher salary range, and a bonus. Large means greater specialization in terms of paralegal assignments. Paralegals become specialists rather than generalists, and salaries for specialists are usually higher than those for generalists.

Of course, there's a downside to working in a large law firm. As with all large organizations, it's difficult to cut through policies and procedures. In other words, it may be easier to negotiate a salary in a small firm than in a large one where salary is tied to a stringent firm policy.

Small law firms. Now let's look at the opposite end of the spectrum. The primary advantage to working in a small firm is the flexibility in assignments and the ambience of the firm—the atmosphere is usually less formal and more relaxed than in large ones. The greatest disadvantage is the limited amount of resources. Most small firms generally don't have word processing or photocopying centers, in-house messengers, a paralegal coordinator/supervisor, an extensive law library, or a senior paralegal career track.

In addition, paralegals in a small firm may have to perform administrative and/or secretarial duties due to budgetary constraints. These tasks may or may not be desirable, depending on personal preferences and career plans. For instance, if you'd like to move into the area of legal administration, some experience performing administrative tasks would be helpful. Small firms can facilitate such cross-experience more easily than large ones. However, be wary of a job that requires you to be both secretary and paralegal. Your salary may be lower and you'll end up performing more clerical tasks than paralegal ones.

Paralegal salaries in small firms may or may not be comparable to those in large firms. Much depends on the attitude of the firm toward paralegals. If the firm is sophisticated in its use of paralegals, the salary will reflect this. On the other hand, if a firm wants to cut costs or doesn't know how to properly utilize paralegals, it won't.

Medium-sized law firms. Many paralegals feel that medium-sized law firms are the best of the lot. They offer the resources of large firms and the flexibility of small firms. Since paralegal turnover in these firms is lower than in the others, these jobs are generally harder to find.

Whatever the size, there's a big difference between working in law firms as opposed to a corporation or government agency: billable hours. The concept of billable hours exists only in law firms, which can make them more of a pressure cooker. However, the positive side to this is that, for the most part, a law firm's environment is more stimulating than a corporation's. In a law firm you work on a variety of cases with a variety of clients. In a corporation, you work for only one client—the corporation.

Corporations

While corporations are the second-largest employer of paralegals, only 15 percent of paralegals find jobs in them. Examples of corporations that employ paralegals include banks, insurance companies, brokerage firms, and manufacturing companies. In a corporation's organizational structure, the legal department usually reports directly to the chief executive officer.

An in-house legal department may consist of anything from a single attorney to over 100, with the average ranging from 1 to 20. The head of the legal department is the general counsel, who may also serve as the corporate secretary. (The title of corporate secretary may be misleading, since the corporate secretary is an officer of the company along with the president and chief financial officer and not a clerical position. In some companies, the corporate secretary is a nonlawyer.) Under the general counsel there are various levels of attorneys, including associate general counsel, assistant general counsel, senior counsel, and counsel. Depending on its size and needs, a legal department may or may not use paralegals.

Since *most* legal departments are too small to handle all the legal work of the corporation, they usually work closely with one or more outside firms. The amount of legal work given to outside counsel depends on the expertise of its in-house legal staff as well as the budgetary constraints of the corporation. (Corporations are also becoming more cost conscious when it comes to their legal bills. As you now know, outside counsel can get pretty expensive.)

A paralegal position in a corporation is significantly different from one in a law firm. One apparent difference—no billable hours—has already been mentioned. After working in a law firm, this can be quite a relief! The second major difference is that there's only one client to keep track of instead of many. As was previously mentioned, while a law firm environment may be stimulating, the pace in the corporation is slow and the pressure is less than in a law firm. This can be great for your mental health!

Another significant difference lies in the duties and responsibilities of paralegals. In a corporation you might be responsible for more business and administrative tasks and less legal research. Also, the tasks performed by a paralegal in a corporation are different from those in a law firm—even within the same specialty area. For instance, one of my responsibilities as a paralegal in a corporation was to administer the company's stock option program, which falls under the legal specialty known as employee benefits. Stock options are a benefit given to key employees and involve the right to buy the company's stock at some time in the future, with luck at a lower price than the market value. Administering the program was very detailed and involved. Before working at the corporation, I had worked in the area of stock options at a law firm where the work involved drafting the agreements for the stock option plans and not administering them. As you can see, the legal specialty area was the same—employee benefits—but the tasks were totally different.

Among the benefits of working at a corporation is the opportunity to learn about other areas of business, such as finance, accounting, and marketing. There are also more opportunities for advancement, since you can apply for positions in other departments. (This is one way to use your paralegal experience as a stepping-stone to other careers. It will be discussed in more detail in Chapter 9.) Corporate salaries and benefits are usually better than those in law firms, although there are always exceptions. In addition, tuition reimbursement is usually included in the benefits package and is a great way to help finance an advanced degree unrelated to law. (Law firms usually provide reimbursement only for seminars and continuing education courses that are directly related to your legal specialty.)

On the downside, positions in corporations are difficult to come by: most hire only paralegals with some law firm experience.

In sum, while corporations offer higher salaries, less stressful environments, and no billable hours, they may not offer the same kind of stimulation and on-the-job variety as law firms.

Government

An alternative to working in a law firm or corporation is a position in a federal, state, or local government agency. Paralegals are employed in federal agencies such as the U.S. Department of Justice, Interstate Commerce Commission, Securities and Exchange Commission, and Federal Trade Commission; in state agencies and state attorneys general's offices; and in district attorney, public defender, and city attorney offices.

In 1975, the federal government developed two job classifications for paralegals: paralegal specialist and legal clerk/technician. Paralegal specialist is considered a professional-level job, which guarantees career mobility and tenure. This job is analogous to the job of a paralegal in private practice who specializes in a particular area. The legal clerk/technician position is similar to a case assistant and is more clerical by nature.

The tasks performed by government paralegals, particularly in the areas of civil and criminal litigation, are similar to those performed by their counterparts in the private sector, including legal and factual research, document analysis/organization, and trial preparation. Public-sector paralegals also have tasks indigenous to government law practice involving regulatory and licensing procedures, administrative hearings, and legislative monitoring.

Before starting her own paralegal placement agency in Minneapolis, Denise Templeton worked in Minnesota's attorney general's office. "I headed its new charitable trust division and was pleasantly surprised," she says. "I expected a typical state government approach by the employees, but instead they were some of the most motivated people I had ever worked with. The work was very interesting, but that really depends on the particular agency you work for. I believe government is a growing sector for paralegal employment. City and county governments are starting to hire experienced paralegals as opposed to bringing employees up through the ranks and calling them something else."

There are other jobs in the federal government that involve paralegal-type work but are not classified that way. They include research analysts at the Federal Trade Commission, equal employment specialists at the Equal Employment Opportunity Commission, and procurement specialists at the Department of Defense. Positions such as these present excellent advancement opportunities.

In 1985, an enlightening study on the employment of paralegals in attorneys general's offices around the nation was conducted by Nancy L. Helmich and Roger A. Larson with the cooperation of the National Association of Attorneys General (NAAG) and the University of Minnesota. Its purpose was to help publicize paralegal career opportunities in public service and to encourage paralegal educational programs to develop curricula in the area of public-sector employment. It showed that paralegals worked in such diverse areas as agriculture, civil rights, consumer affairs, criminal law, education, environmental affairs, health, labor, natural resources, public safety, taxation, transportation, and welfare, to name a few. Perhaps the most interesting aspect of the study was information on the reasons why paralegals chose public-sector employment. A common answer was interest in public affairs and issues related to government service. Other responses included the challenge and variety offered by public service and the opportunity to help people and serve the public.

While a paralegal position in a government agency may be interesting, it should be noted that less than 5 percent of all paralegals work in this capacity. There are several reasons for this. The most obvious concerns the problem of bureaucratic red tape. Any government job involves extensive civil service procedures that have to be followed. Sometimes this results in long delays in obtaining employment, which can be quite frustrating. Second, since the government doesn't bill clients for services, the argument for cost-effectiveness that's used for paralegals in the private sector doesn't apply. And, because only a small number of paralegals are employed in the public sector, their talents and skills are likely to be underutilized by the attorneys who work with them.

If the government is to continue providing low-cost legal services to the poor, the elderly, and others, it is apparent that both lawyers and paralegals need to focus greater attention on the role of paralegals in public service. In addition, more paralegal training programs should include courses on the public-sector paralegal. There is some irony in the fact that while less than 5 percent of all paralegals are employed by the government, the government, as an industry, was the first to recognize the benefits of using them.

For anyone considering a paralegal position with the federal government, I recommend obtaining a copy of a pamphlet entitled "The Paralegal's Guide to U.S. Government Jobs: How to Land a Job in 70 Law-Related Careers," available from Federal Reports, Inc., in Washington, D.C. It provides detailed information on the pros and cons of federal employment and on the application and hiring process and a list of agencies, job titles, and salary ranges.

As more and more government agencies come to recognize the value of using paralegals, opportunities for paralegal employment in the public sector will increase. Nevertheless, due to the nature of our legal system, the greatest number of paralegal jobs will continue to be found in law firms.

Other Organizations

In recent years, paralegals have found employment in nonprofit agencies, legal clinics, group legal services, consumer groups, and paralegal service companies. This is due to the demand for affordable legal services and increased recognition of paralegals by employers other than law firms and corporations.

Paralegal service companies are a recent phenomenon. They are usually owned and operated exclusively by paralegals or former paralegals. They provide legal support for law firms in the areas of civil litigation, family, probate, corporate, business, and bankruptcy law, to name a few; employment opportunities for recent paralegal graduates; and internship possibilities for students currently enrolled in paralegal programs.

The Eden Council for Hope & Opportunity (ECHO), located in Hayward, California, is an example of a nontraditional work environment for paralegals. ECHO was incorporated in 1964 to combat housing discrimination by providing services in the areas of tenant rights and responsibilities, conciliation, and mediation; rent subsidy program counseling; and information, referral, educational, and outreach services. It employs nonlawyers to provide counseling services in the areas of rent, security deposits, harassment, invasion of privacy, property maintenance, and eviction and mediation services regarding rental disputes. When ECHO nonlawyer Steve Wagner spoke at a recent paralegal career seminar, he made it clear that he thoroughly enjoyed his work. It gave him the opportunity to help people in need and perform fulfilling community service work.

While the organizations mentioned here represent alternative employment opportunities for paralegals, less than 5 percent of paralegals find positions in them. It is hoped that this will change as the legal industry creates alternative methods for the delivery of cost-effective legal services. One more thing: the salary level for paralegal positions in these organizations is generally substantially lower than in law firms, corporations, and government agencies.

Now that you've looked at several kinds of paralegal employers, the next two chapters will examine the job responsibilities and duties of paralegals in the major legal specialty areas.

Chapter

What Do Paralegals Do?
Part 1: Legal Research and Litigation

The successful people are the ones who can think up stuff for the rest of the world to keep busy at.

Don Marquis

A paralegal sits cross-legged on the floor of a large room that's stacked to the ceiling with dozens of boxes. The boxes are filled with thousands of documents. Head bent, the paralegal is stamping the documents and preparing an index of each box. This image of a paralegal poring over a roomful of endless documents is outdated and changing. It's been replaced by the vision of a new, more sophisticated paralegal performing tasks that were once the exclusive domain of attorneys.

While stamping and indexing documents manually is still done for some cases, it's not done for the largest of them, and it's not required by every practice area. The tasks paralegals perform—with the exception of one—depend largely on the area of law they're in and whom they work for. The exception is legal research. It's a vital part of almost every area of law, and something every paralegal should know how to do.

The four areas of law that 90 percent of all paralegals work in are litigation, corporate, real estate, and estate planning/probate. Of those paralegals, more than 50 percent work in litigation. Because litigation is the resolution of disputes between two or more parties that are enforceable in court, the responsibilities of paralegals in this field are heavily weighted toward lawsuits and the courts—in other practice areas they are not. Criminal law and family law are also included in this chapter, since the tasks performed by paralegals in these areas are similar to those in litigation.

As such, I believe legal research and litigation are the best areas to use to introduce you to some of the things paralegals do on the job: summarizing documents, Shepardizing, organizing files, and conducting interviews, to name a few. But first, and bear with me on this, you'll need some background on the law and the way our legal system is set up.

The Law in Brief

Laws are the principles that govern conduct, protect rights, and define responsibilities. They're based on centuries of accumulated custom and theory and serve society by providing a framework for governing the relationships and transactions that occur in daily life. They help to resolve disputes and maintain order.

Much of the law in the United States is based on the legal principles that were in effect under British rule—called common law—before the American Revolution. Interestingly, much of British common law was influenced by ancient Roman law. On these borrowed, inherited, and refined principles, the U.S. legal system is composed of four layers of law: constitutional law, statutory law, case law, and administrative law.

Laws are made through amendments to the U.S. Constitution and to the constitutions of each of the fifty states *(constitutional law)*; through the passage of statutes by the U.S. Congress and by state and local legislatures *(statutory law)*; through decisions made in federal, state, and local courts *(case law)*; and through the passage of rules, regulations, orders, and decisions, such as Internal Revenue Service rulings, by federal, state, and local administrative agencies *(administrative law)*.

Case law is a written opinion that explains a court decision and is based on precedent—the idea that that which came before affects what comes after. A court uses precedent when, after applying specific legal principles to a case with a certain set of facts, it adheres to those principles by applying them in the future to cases with substantially the same facts.

Cases may be argued in three levels of court. The first level is *trial* court. In it, a case is heard, its facts determined by the judge or jury, and law applied to those facts by the judge. (In a jury trial, however, the judge would instruct the jury as to what legal principles it should apply.) Once the law is applied, a judgment is made. If the judgment is appealed by either of the parties in the case (appeals can be made only on questions of law), the matter goes to the next level of court—an *appellate* court. The appellate court determines whether the ruling and judgment of the trial court were correct, and it issues an opinion. If either of the parties wishes to appeal this opinion, the case is forwarded to a *supreme*, or high, court. The high court reviews the determination of the appellate court and issues an opinion that affirms or rejects the appellate decision.

Other, special courts also exist at federal, state, and local levels. They include Tax Court, Court of Patent Appeals, Small Claims Court, Probate Court, Family Court, and Juvenile Court.

Two kinds of cases often brought to court are criminal and civil (actions between private parties). They represent two major kinds of law. Criminal law is designed to protect the public at large and deals with actions society deems harmful to the public welfare. In criminal law, government takes the responsibility for prosecuting the individual.

Civil law is designed to protect citizens as private individuals in their relationships with one another. The majority of civil lawsuits revolve around contracts or torts. A contract is a written or unwritten agreement (a promise or set of promises) between two or more parties. A tort—a wrong or injury to a person or damage to property—is the principle through which the injured party can collect monetary compensation from the person who caused the harm. Most torts involve wrongdoing to individuals under civil law, although torts do arise from criminal actions, such as assault and battery.

I hope that this information will make it easier for you to understand how different aspects of the law relate to the various practice areas and, ultimately, how they affect the duties and responsibilities of paralegals in those fields.

Legal Research

There are some tasks that are so elemental to the nature of the practice of law that paralegals in every practice area do them. They include conducting interviews with clients to gather background information; acting as liaison between clients, agencies, courts, and lawyers; preparing correspondence to clients, lawyers, and administrative agencies; drafting legal documents; analyzing, summarizing, and indexing documents; monitoring laws relevant to their specialty area; organizing and maintaining files; and conducting legal and factual research. Simply put, paralegals spend most of their time reading, writing, and researching. Of all these tasks, legal research is among the most essential. This section focuses on the kinds of research conducted by paralegals who work in the area of litigation.

Searching for Legal Authorities

Conducting legal research isn't difficult—it just takes some getting used to. Its foundation is the search for authorities in the law that are applicable to the facts of a particular legal problem or situation. The authorities are used to make an argument in court.

Authorities are found in either primary or secondary sources. Primary sources are actual laws: statutes passed by federal, state, and local legislatures (found in code books); court decisions (found in case books that are also known as reports or reporters); and administrative rules, regulations, and decisions. Secondary authorities aren't law. They're statements about the law and consist of two types: books of search, such as encyclopedias, legal periodicals, and textbooks that explain or describe the law, and books of index, such as digests, form books, tables, and dictionaries that are used to locate the law.

The search for authorities always begins with a search for mandatory primary sources, that is, constitutional, statutory, or case law of the same jurisdiction as your case. If these can't be found, then the search would move to persuasive primary sources—court decisions from other jurisdictions. Mandatory sources are key to any case because the judge who hears the case must consider or apply law of the same jurisdiction to the facts of it. Persuasive sources can serve to guide the judge if the law those sources point to is relevant to the case at hand.

Before attempting a search for authorities, a paralegal must know two things: the facts of the case and the legal issues involved in it. This information is usually obtained from an attorney. Once a paralegal understands the facts and issues, he or she can use several methods to conduct the search.

Finding the law. When researching a legal problem, you need the key words or phrases that will lead you to the right primary authorities. This is called the word approach to finding the law (though it's sometimes called the subject or the topical approach). One way to identify key words is to look at the problem in terms of four elements:

- *Subject matter*—What things or places are involved?

- *People*—Do the parties involved fit into a particular group of people that may be important to the outcome of the lawsuit?
- *Legal theory*—What kinds of claims and defenses are being made?
- *Relief*—What does the person initiating the lawsuit want?

Let's say that your firm's client, Mr. Smith, was out on his morning 5-mile run. Part of that run takes him through the property of Mr. Jones, his neighbor. While Smith was on Jones's property, Pooch, Jones's dog, rushed up to Smith, causing Smith to trip, fall, and injure his ankle. His medical bills total $1,500. Smith sues Jones for damages for injuries. Can Smith collect?

In this example, the key words for the four elements might be property and animal (subject matter), property owner and trespasser (people), tort and negligence and trespassing (legal theory), and damages for medical expenses (relief).

Once the key words have been identified, there are several types of secondary source law books that index the law on the basis of subject matter, words, and topics. These sources refer you to specific cases and discussions on the points of law regarding your legal problem.

If you already know the name of a specific case, you can skip the word approach and go directly to it. A case is customarily referred to in terms of volume, source, and page number. The notation used to indicate these terms is called the cite (short for citation) and looks like this:

Ullman v. United States, 350. U.S. 422 (1956)

Deciphered, this cite means Ullman is the plaintiff; United States is the defendant; 350 is the volume number; U.S. is the abbreviation for the title of the publication, in this case, *United States Supreme Court Reports;* 422 is the page on which the case is found; and 1956 is the year it was decided. Once you become familiar with this reference system, locating cases is easy.

As stated earlier, case law is the written opinion that explains a decision made by a court. For research purposes, it can be found in either official reports published or authorized by the government or unofficial reports published by a private legal publishing company. The most popular unofficial publication of federal, regional, and state opinions is called West's National Reporter System. West has devised a unique key numbering system that it uses for all its publications. With it, legal principles are broken down into subject areas and subcategories and assigned key numbers. Related cases are correspondingly referenced under the same numbers. Because key number assignments are used in all of West's publications, they can help to locate cases that pertain to a particular subject or legal principle easily throughout the Reporter System.

Administrative agency decisions, opinions, rules, and regulations are published by private legal publishers in what are known as loose-leaf reports. (They are so named because they consist of separate, individual pages that can be inserted and removed from loose-leaf binders.) Commerce Clearing House (CCH) publishes various loose-leaf reports on tax law. Matthew Bender is another well-known legal publisher of loose-leaf reports. These reports also cite statutes and case law.

Shepardizing—Is the Law Valid?

Suppose you have found five cases that support Mr. Smith's argument. Or do they? How do you know if these cases are still law or whether they were reversed or overruled last month by an appellate or high court? Have the courts followed the principles of law established in the case? Before you can use a case as authority for the client's argument, you need to know how it was treated by the courts.

The method for doing that is called Shepardizing, named after Frank Shepard, who invented the system in 1873. *Shepard's Citations*, published by Shepard's/McGraw-Hill, are a set of books that include cases, federal and state statutes, administrative agency rulings, and material from legal periodicals. Through a notation system that takes some getting used to, *Shepard's* provides the history of a case (whether it was affirmed, dismissed, modified, reversed, or vacated) and its treatment (whether it was explained, followed, overruled, or questioned). Shepardizing is usually done by paralegals, although some attorneys prefer to do it themselves.

While a detailed discussion of how to Shepardize is beyond the scope of this book, suffice it to say that Shepardizing is one of the most essential tools of legal research. The consequences of improper Shepardizing can be devastating. Imagine an attorney walking into a courtroom only to find out that the cases he or she used in order to prepare—the cases *you* Shepardized—have been reversed. I've seen it happen.

Legal Research Assignments

The kinds of legal research done by paralegals vary widely, depending on the practice area they are in. A tax paralegal may use a law library differently from a litigation paralegal, for instance.

Typical litigation-related assignments would be to photocopy, cite check, and/or Shepardize cases; prepare a memorandum of law; and obtain information from computerized legal research databases such as WESTLAW or LEXIS (the last is explained in more detail in chapter 7). Rarely will an attorney ask a paralegal to conduct substantive legal research, that is, finding cases "on point" that could help or hinder a client's argument. With so much at stake, lawyers generally do these themselves.

Litigation: A Primary Practice Area

Since dispute resolution is the most common function of law in our legal system, it should come as no surprise that more than half of all paralegals work in litigation. As stated earlier, litigation refers to a controversy in which all parties agree to have their legal rights determined and enforced in court. In a strict technical sense, the term refers to civil actions and not to criminal actions.

As you read on, keep in mind that in order to discuss the responsibilities of each practice area, it's necessary for me to use legal terms and concepts that may be unfamiliar to you. It isn't my intention to bog you down with terminology, but rather to introduce them to you as some of the things paralegals should know. The boxed features in this chapter and Chapter 4 will provide you with some definitions. However, if you have difficulty with any terms that aren't included in the boxes, there are several good legal dictionaries and paralegal handbooks available that will define them.

Recall that most civil actions pertain to a dispute involving a contract or a tort between individuals, corporations, or both. Because tort litigation often involves cases in which personal injuries are due to auto accidents, medical malpractice, and products liability, the tasks performed by paralegals in that area are more than likely to center on people, places, and things that relate to the medical and health-care fields.

What Is a Lawsuit?

Since nearly all of the duties performed by litigation paralegals revolve around lawsuits, a little background on the processes and procedures of them is necessary. There are four stages to a lawsuit: commencement of an action (complaint and answer), discovery, trial, and appeal.

The first phase begins when one party files a complaint against another. The complaint is the first statement (or pleading) prepared by whoever is initiating the lawsuit (the plaintiff) and deals with the nature and basis of the lawsuit (the grounds). Its purpose is to notify the adversary, or defendant, of the grounds for the suit. The defendant then prepares an answer in response, which contains denials of the allegations made by the plaintiff. A law firm would represent either the plaintiff or the defendant.

The second phase is called discovery. This is where both parties literally discover facts and information about the other. There are four tools used for discovery.

- *Interrogatories*—A fancy term for written questions.

- *Depositions*—Statements made under oath in a question-and-answer format.

- *Requests for production of documents*—A request by one party that the other party produce documents for it and make them available for inspection and photocopying.

- *Requests for admissions*—Written statements that positively affirm or deny facts or allegations at issue in the case. (These serve two purposes: to uncover facts and to resolve some issues before going to trial.)

The third phase, the trial, is an examination of the issues and facts of a case in a court that has jurisdiction over it. Trial procedures include jury selection (if it's a trial by jury), the attorneys' opening statements, the plaintiff's presentation of evidence, the defendant's objections, the defendant's presentation of evidence, the plaintiff's objections, submission of the case to a jury, instructions to the jury, the verdict, and order of the court.

The fourth stage of a lawsuit is the appeal to a higher court. Both the plaintiff and the defendant have the right to file an appeal—within a specified time period—if not satisfied with the verdict. The purpose of the appeal is to obtain a review of a lower court's decision and a reversal of the judgment or a new trial. The appellate court bases its decision primarily on the attorneys' written pleadings and not on their oral arguments.

┌─── **Selected Litigation Terminology** ───┐

Brief— A written statement, presented to a court or administrative agency, that outlines the essential principles of law that should be applied to a client's case. The statement is supported by legal citations and authorities gathered mainly through legal research.

Jury instructions—The instructions given by the judge to a jury (if there is one) informing the jurors of the law applicable to the facts of the case.

Pleading—The formal written document that states the position of a litigant in a lawsuit.

Posttrial collections work—The business of collecting the funds owed to the attorney, such as client fees, after the trial has been completed. Posttrial collection work may also involve all the legal procedures and paperwork required to collect an award granted by the court to a client.

Settlement conference—A conference held before the court renders a final judgment, at which the plaintiff and defendant seek a compromise settlement of the issues in dispute in the lawsuit.

The Litigation Paralegal's Job

To reiterate, the tasks performed by any paralegal vary greatly depending on the type of organization, the size of the case, the complexity of the legal issues, the level of the paralegal's experience, and the attitude of the attorney supervising the paralegal. The tasks discussed here are typical for paralegals working on small- to medium-sized civil litigation cases at law firms that involve paralegals in cases from beginning to end. (It's worth noting that paralegals hired to work on large, complex cases often work only on discovery. Since discovery on these kinds of cases can take years, it's common for a paralegal to change jobs or leave the firm before the case ever goes to trial.)

Commencement of an action. In the first phase of a lawsuit—the commencement of an action—a paralegal would be responsible for:

- Performing investigation and analysis of the facts of the case
- Organizing and analyzing client documents
- Preparing chronologies of facts in the case
- Drafting or assisting in drafting the complaint or answer (if representing the plaintiff or defendant, respectively)

- Setting up and maintaining a calendar system
- Performing legal or factual research

Discovery. The next part of the lawsuit, discovery, is where a paralegal would spend most of his or her time.

- Preparing interrogatories, requests for production of documents, and requests for admissions and/or responses to these documents
- Drafting motions (formal requests to the judge relating to issues that arise during the lawsuit)
- Locating, interviewing, and obtaining witness statements
- Drafting deposition questions
- Organizing files and analyzing documents
- Supervising a computerized litigation support system (if applicable)
- Summarizing depositions
- Managing document productions

Of all these tasks, summarizing depositions and managing document productions are the most time-consuming. A deposition summary is a summary, in the summarizer's own words, of testimony taken in a deposition. For instance, the attorney you've been assigned to has spent the last three days taking Mr. Doe's deposition. A transcript of it has been typed up by a court reporter and is 500 pages long. It would be too time-consuming for the attorney to read through all 500 pages to prepare for trial, so you're responsible for condensing it into a 40-page summary. (On average, it takes an hour to summarize 15 pages of transcript.)

Deposition summaries can be nearly unmanageable when hundreds of volumes of transcripts need to be summarized. In these cases, depositions are sometimes—though rarely—sent out to a deposition summary service. I've found that due to the confidential nature of the testimony, most firms prefer to have their own paralegals do the summaries. Summarizing hundreds of volumes is an enormous task and often leads to very frustrated paralegals.

The other task that takes up a lot of time is preparing for document productions. A document production is a legal device used by both sides of a suit to discover the facts in a case. For example, let's say that the firm you work for is representing the IBM Corporation, the plaintiff in a case. Your attorney has just received a request from the defendant for all of IBM's documents that refer in any way to the Xerox Corporation from 1970 to 1984. It's your job as a paralegal to go through all of the documents that have been received from the client, locate the ones that refer to Xerox in that time period, and make them available to the defendant for inspection. It's likely that you'd have to examine thousands of documents to complete a task like this, and it's possible that it would take hundreds of hours.

A time will be set for the defendant's attorney to inspect the documents (usually at your firm). After the attorney has decided which document he or she wants, you would arrange for copies of those documents to be made and sent to that attorney's office. (If you were a paralegal working for the defendant, once your attorney received those documents, you would be responsible for stamping them with a Bates number, putting them in chronological order, and preparing an index of all the documents.) No matter what side of the case you're working for, managing documents is time-consuming.

One more thing: document requests continue throughout the discovery phase of the lawsuit. As a result, some of the larger cases have dozens of document productions. Once again, this is a frustrating job for some paralegals. And yet, discovery can be quite interesting—particularly in small cases where there are few depositions and documents to manage.

Trial. A paralegal's responsibilities during the trial phase of a lawsuit fall into three categories—pretrial, trial, and posttrial. Some of the assignments might include:

- *Pretrial*—Drafting legal documents such as briefs, pretrial statements, settlement conference memoranda, and jury instructions
  —Reviewing briefs for accuracy of factual information
  —Shepardizing and cite checking
  —Preparing trial exhibits and trial notebook
  —Obtaining a list of jury members
- *Trial*—Coordinating the scheduling of witnesses
  —Assisting in the preparation of witnesses
  —Attending the trial and taking notes
  —Maintaining a list of exhibits
- *Posttrial*—Summarizing trial testimony
  —Preparing a bill of costs
  —Drafting a motion for a new trial (if applicable)
  —Managing posttrial collections work

Trials represent the culmination of months, sometimes years, of hard work and can be quite rewarding (if your side wins, of course). But they are also a time of tremendous stress; everyone puts in overtime.

Appeal. The final phase of the lawsuit, the appeal, is based primarily on the pleadings submitted by the attorneys and not on oral arguments. Since the majority of time required by a lawsuit is spent on discovery, very few paralegals ever perform appellate work.

In the following statement, Ingrid Tronsrue, a litigation paralegal at Davis, Graham & Stubbs in Denver, Colorado, describes her responsibilities and the things she likes about her job. "My job consists a great deal of trial work, document organization and control, and talking with codefendants and the plaintiff's counsel. I love going to trial. I'm currently working with twenty-one plaintiffs and five codefendants on a products liability case that involves very complex medical issues. [Products liability cases typically involve claims that a product was defective—in some way due to negligent manufacture—and resulted in an injury.] I spend a lot of time working with expert witnesses, coordinating the scheduling of medical exams for the plaintiffs, as well as scheduling the depositions. Essentially, I make sure everything flows smoothly and that the attorneys have what they need. At this firm, most of the legal research is done by law clerks, but, with all the other responsibilities I have, I don't miss it. What I enjoy most is dealing with people, working with our investigator, and calling the expert witnesses myself and interviewing them." This kind of hands-on involvement is considered by many paralegals to be one of the main advantages of working in litigation.

Computerized Litigation: An Emerging Specialty

During the past decade, a new litigation subspecialty has emerged to provide an answer to the problem of document management for very large cases and, in the process, has opened up new job opportunities for paralegals interested in computers. As you'll read in Chapter 7, computerized litigation support systems manage, access, and retrieve information and documents in a fraction of the time required by manual systems. Computerized systems are particularly efficient during discovery, when thousands of documents may need to be organized, indexed, and coded for retrieval at a moment's notice. They are costly, however, and generally used by the larger law firms.

In computerized litigation support, a paralegal's responsibilities would include:

- Analyzing and selecting the hardware and software components of the computer system
- Acting as liaison between the attorney and the computer programmer
- Acting as project manager (which includes supervising other paralegals, scheduling timetables, and coordinating assignments)
- Acting as systems manager (which includes supervising backup and maintenance procedures)
- Training other support staff in the use of the system

Chyllene Cattie, a paralegal at Dechert, Price and Rhoads in Philadelphia, describes her responsibilities in this area: "A partner will tell me that he needs a database to do this or that. It's up to me to figure out how to do those things. I sit down with a computer programmer, figure out the needs of the attorney, and help design the program by making it applicable to that particular case. I hire temporary paralegals, usually graduates of local paralegal programs, to perform data entry. They extract information from documents that correlates to the specific fields in the software program that we have identified as important and relevant to the issues in the case. I'm also responsible for generating various reports from the system once it's designed."

Criminal Law

Criminal law is a specialty area that most people are familiar with thanks to "Perry Mason" and "L.A. Law." But, while television has popularized it, in reality, fewer paralegals work in this area than in civil litigation. While some of the tasks performed by paralegals who work in criminal law are similar to the tasks that are done in civil litigation, criminal law is generally considered a specialty in itself. Criminal law paralegals are also responsible for knowing about criminal procedures, such as arrest, search, seizure, warrants, bail, pleas, confession, and probation and for differentiating between the various types of crimes, such as petty offenses, misdemeanors, and felonies.

Before I explain the tasks of a criminal law paralegal, I'd like to give you some background. Recall that one of the functions of law in our society is to help maintain order. Criminal laws are statutes enacted by legislatures to preserve the public order. The statutes define offenses against the public and impose penalties for violations.

Once a crime has been committed and the suspect arrested and booked (the charge against him or her entered in the police station's charge book), the suspect is brought before a judge. At this preliminary examination, the judge reviews the complaint and the evidence. If the judge decides the evidence is insufficient, the case is dismissed. If not, the case is turned over to a prosecutor or a grand jury, depending on the state in which the crime occurred. A grand jury is a panel of citizens that decides whether or not the defendant will stand trial. Both the grand jury and the prosecutor can indict the suspect and order him or her to stand trial if they find the evidence convincing.

The next step in the proceedings is the arraignment. At an arraignment, a judge reads the charges to the defendant, who then enters a plea. The most common pleas are guilty, not guilty, and not guilty by reason of insanity. If the defendant pleads guilty, the matter is set for sentencing. If the plea is not guilty, a date for trial is set.

After the trial, depending on the verdict, either the case is dismissed or the defendant is ordered to return for sentencing or a motion is made for a new trial or an appeal is filed.

In criminal law, some of a paralegal's assignments would include:

- Interviewing police officers and witnesses regarding the alleged crime
- Arranging for laboratory examination of evidence
- Taking photographs of things, places, or people related to the alleged crime
- Assisting in making bail arrangements
- Obtaining police reports, search warrants, and information for plea bargaining
- Preparing charges or pleas for arraignment
- Making preparations for the preliminary hearing or grand jury presentation
- Preparing sentencing information
- Examining physical evidence
- Working as liaison between the client and probation officer

┌── **Selected Criminal Law Terminology** ──┐

Felony—A serious crime, usually punishable by imprisonment or death.

Indictment—A document prepared by a district attorney and submitted to a grand jury that charges a party with the commission of a crime.

Misdemeanor—A type of criminal offense that is less serious than a felony, such as trespassing, involving less serious penalties than a felony.

Petty offense—A minor violation of criminal law, such as jaywalking, less serious than either a misdemeanor or felony. There are minor penalties for petty offenses, typically a fine rather than a jail sentence.

Family Law

The practice area of family law includes divorce, custody, child support, and adoption. Paralegals who work in this field need to understand the laws that pertain to adoption, marriage, nuptial agreements, legal separations, annulments, divorce, child support, alimony, and property matters (such as community property and equitable distribution), among many other things. Of course, some of the tasks family law paralegals perform are similar to those done by the paralegals who work in litigation, because family law matters occasionally involve court- and trial-related activities. As with criminal law, however, family law is a specialty area separate from the practice area of litigation.

A big part of a family law practice is divorce. Divorce proceedings are made up of several phases: commencement of an action by filing a petition, preparation of motions for temporary orders or injunctions, assessment of a client's financial status, discovery, negotiation of property or support settlements, trial or hearing (if settlement negotiations are unsuccessful), and preparation of documents for the transfer of property.

Paralegals in this area would be responsible for:

- Gathering background information on the client (sources of support, assets, number of children, and residence, for example)
- Drafting legal documents (petitions for the dissolution of

marriage, motions for temporary restraining orders, property settlement agreements, decrees of dissolution, and petitions to modify child support, among them)

- Determining support needs and calculating child support
- Arranging for appraisal of personal and real property
- Assisting the client in the preparation of income and expense reports
- Preparing documents for transfer of assets
- Gathering data for a petition to adopt
- Preparing a petition for adoption

It's worth noting that there's a great deal of emotional stress involved in both criminal law and family law. If you're contemplating becoming a paralegal in either of these areas, some course work in psychology and sociology is recommended.

Selected Family Law Terminology

Annulment—A court declaration that a marriage was invalid from the outset.

Community property—All the property that spouses jointly acquire by their efforts during marriage. Some states hold that, in the event of divorce, the spouses are entitled to equal division of the marital property.

Decree of dissolution—In family law, the final court-approved order that dissolves marital bonds between husband and wife.

Equitable distribution—In family law, the fair and just distribution of the marital property acquired by the spouses. Unlike community property, the property is not necessarily distributed in equal amounts to the spouses.

Nuptial agreement—An agreement entered into by husband and wife before marriage that details each other's rights in the event of divorce or death.

Petition—A written request that the court take some corrective action to give a petitioning party some remedy or relief.

Property settlement agreement—A formal agreement that divides the marital property between the spouses.

Temporary restraining order—A court order that forbids an action or threatened action by a party until the court can hold a hearing on the matter. In family law, for example, this order might be issued to bar one spouse from disposing of assets.

If you do become a paralegal, chances are that your first position will be in litigation. If you think you'll thrive in an adversarial atmosphere, it is a good place to start. If not, litigation isn't the only field open to you. To fully answer the question "What do paralegals do?", the next chapter examines some of the practice areas that don't involve lawsuits. Indeed, some of these areas require paralegals to use even more sophisticated skills and training than does litigation.

Chapter

4

What Do Paralegals Do?
Part 2: Specialty Areas That Do Not Focus on Lawsuits

Discourage litigation. Persuade your neighbor to compromise whenever you can. As a peacemaker the lawyer has a superior opportunity of being a good man.

Abraham Lincoln

For most people, hearing the words "law" and "lawyer" conjures up strong images of lawsuits, trials, juries, and judges. Seldom do they think of the side of the law that doesn't revolve around the courtroom. But practice areas such as corporate, real estate, intellectual property, and labor law are just as much a part of the legal profession as litigation.

In fact, the laws that govern these practice areas are what provide the framework for regulating the (hopefully) nonadversarial relationships and transactions of daily life. They cover matters such as incorporation, mergers and acquisitions, real estate purchases and sales, wills, estate management, workers' compensation, and trademark registration, to name a few. For the most part, they don't involve litigation, courtrooms, or lawsuits. One thing is for sure, though, they do provide many good employment opportunities for paralegals.

In 1981, after a year of working in civil litigation at a large San Francisco law firm, I knew litigation wasn't for me. It occurred to me that there was only so much I could do as a paralegal in that field. Furthermore, I wasn't too thrilled with the adversarial nature of it. After making my feelings known to the firm's paralegal manager, I switched into the securities and corporate group. The difference in jobs was like night and day. I no longer had to deal with courts, trials, or deposition summaries. For the next eight years, I worked exclusively in various nonlitigation areas. I've never regretted the move.

The purpose of this chapter is to let you know that, contrary to the popular belief held by the general public and some paralegals, there are *many* areas of law that don't involve litigation. It discusses a few of those areas—corporate, securities, real estate, estate planning/probate, bankruptcy, intellectual property, and labor law—what they involve and what responsibilities a paralegal working in them may have.

Corporate Law: A Primary Practice Area

Approximately 15–20 percent of all paralegals work in corporate law. Since corporate law revolves around business-related transactions, paralegals in this specialty area rarely perform court-related tasks. (Depending on your personal preferences, this is either an advantage or disadvantage.) Their work most often relates to incorporations, ongoing corporate matters, mergers and acquisitions, dissolving corporations, and partnership matters.

Incorporations

Incorporation is the legal process through which an association of owners creates a corporation; that is, it's a way of structuring a company. The process is governed by state statutes. The legal document that establishes a corporation is called the articles of incorporation. A corporation is considered an artificial person under the law and exists as a legal entity separate from the people who own it. Those people, the shareholders, elect directors to manage the affairs of the organization. The directors, in turn, appoint officers to run the day-to-day operations.

The principal benefit of a corporation as a framework for a business is that it limits the liability of its shareholders. Essentially, this means that, because it's a separate entity, a corporation can be sued in its own name, not in the names of its shareholders. In that way, the shareholders' personal assets can't be seized if the corporation defaults on a loan. (In contrast, the owners and/or partners of sole proprietorships and partnerships—two other ways of structuring a business—*are* personally liable for the debts of their companies.)

Corporate paralegals who work on an incorporation are responsible for:

- Determining the availability of the corporate name and reserving it with the secretary of state
- Drafting and filing articles of incorporation
- Drafting the bylaws, minutes of first meeting of the board of directors and shareholders, and answers for various federal and state forms
- Preparing the minutes book, share certificates, stock transfer records, and qualifications for issuance of stock
- Obtaining appropriate licenses to operate specific businesses, such as a liquor store, hotel, or pharmacy, when necessary

As a corporate paralegal in a law firm, I prepared dozens of incorporations. In contrast, after four years of working in law departments at various corporations, I prepared only one incorporation. Remember, paralegals who are employed by law firms work for a variety of clients as opposed to those employed by corporations, who work for one client, the corporation itself.

Ongoing Corporate Matters

The duties that are performed by paralegals and related to the ongoing maintenance of a corporation vary considerably, depending in large part on whether the paralegal works in a law firm or corporation. For a paralegal working in a law firm, the tasks generally include:

- Drafting legal documents, such as employment agreements, shareholders' agreements, and stock option plans
- Amending articles of incorporation and/or bylaws
- Preparing notices, agendas, resolutions, and minutes for corcorporate activities that require the approval of directors and/or shareholders
- Filing the qualifications for corporations to do business in other states
- Maintaining corporate records of subsidiaries
- Preparing Uniform Commercial Code (UCC) filings. (The UCC is a set of laws that govern commercial transactions between states.)

In addition to these duties, paralegals who work for corporations may have responsibilities that revolve around the activities of the corporate secretary and board of directors. These include:

- Reporting the purchase and sale of stock by officers and directors
- Preparing for board of directors meetings
- Calculating dividend record and payable dates
- Administering executive stock option programs and dividend reinvestment plans
- Drafting proxy statements and 10-K forms
- Managing shareholder relations programs and proxy solicitations
- Supervising the stock transfer agent
- Coordinating the annual meeting of shareholders

Selected Corporate and Securities Law Terminology

Bylaws—The rules that govern the day-to-day internal affairs of a corporation.

Certificate of election to dissolve and wind up—A document indicating that a corporation's board of directors, with the approval of voting shareholders, has elected to dissolve a corporation.

Form 10-K—A document that discloses a corporation's total revenues, expenses, and operating income filed with the Securities and Exchange Commission (SEC) annually by the corporation.

Form 10-Q—A document similar to the 10-K, but filed quarterly with the SEC.

Letter of intent—A nonbinding letter that expresses the intention of parties to enter into a binding agreement regarding a specific matter, such as the merger or acquisition of a business, at some future time.

Notice to creditors—A notice to inform creditors that a company is about to dissolve, so that the creditors can post claims against the company.

Registration statements—The submission of financial information to the SEC so that a business can buy and sell stocks and/or bonds in the stock market.

Underwriting agreement—An agreement by an underwriter, usually a brokerage house, to market the securities of a firm for a fee.

Mergers and Acquisitions

Due to the wave of corporate takeovers that occurred in the mid-1980s, the attorneys and paralegals who worked on these transactions developed specialized knowledge in the area of mergers and acquisitions (also known as M&A). The responsibilities of a paralegal who works in mergers and acquisitions might include:

- Assisting in drafting letters of intent
- Preparing drafts of merger, purchase, and sale agreements
- Participating in due diligence investigations
- Drafting employment contracts and closing documents
- Obtaining UCC filing clearances and good standing certificates

Kathy Allen, a paralegal at Sutherland, Asbill & Brennan in Atlanta, Georgia, works in M&A. She comments below on some of her responsibilities. Note her career path and educational background. It's typical of those who work in this area of corporate law.

"I started in general corporate and gradually moved into securities work, particularly in the area of mergers and acquisitions. I do a great deal of research to make sure the company is qualified to do business in all the states. I also perform due diligence, which is done when a company becomes public or is involved in an acquisition. It consists of reviewing company records to make sure they are in proper order and that the company is in good standing. I have found my bachelor's degree in finance to be useful, particularly when doing due diligence, reading annual reports, and helping attorneys interpret the financial status of a particular company."

One final note about M&A work. It's a subspecialty of corporate and securities law, and paralegal jobs in it are few and far between.

Corporate Dissolutions

Corporate paralegals who work on dissolving corporations would be assigned to draft, file, and obtain documents in connection with certificates of election to wind up and dissolve; statements of intent to dissolve, articles of dissolution, and other required state forms to effect dissolution; notices to creditors; tax clearances; withdrawals of qualifications to do business in other states; state and federal tax dissolution forms; distribution of corporate assets; and cancellation of share certificates.

Partnerships

As mentioned earlier, a partnership is another way to structure a company. It is a mutual agreement, either written or verbal, between two or more persons to carry on a business for profit. The most common type of partnership is a limited partnership, usually formed for real estate purchases and for oil or gas drilling ventures. It consists of one or more general partners, who manage the partnership, and limited partners, who only contribute capital. Limited partners don't participate in the operation or management of the partnership and are liable only for the amount of their investment.

The duties of paralegals within the area of partnerships vary depending on the law at any given time. For instance, in the early 1980s, when tax laws favored partnerships, I found myself spending 80 percent of my time working on partnership transactions. When the tax laws changed, I spent most of my time preparing incorporations.

In partnership transactions, a paralegal's responsibilities would include:

- Drafting general or limited partnership agreements and amendments
- Preparing, filing, and recording statements of partnership and certificates of limited partnership
- Preparing, filing, and publishing fictitious business name statements (if the partnership is to operate under an assumed name and not under the partners' actual names) and notices of termination of partnership
- Drafting minutes of partnership meetings and agreements for dissolution of partnership

Securities Law

Securities law is a subspecialty of corporate law. As such, there are no hard figures on the number of paralegals who work exclusively in it; those paralegals are included in the figures for corporate law. Securities law involves the sale and purchase of securities—stocks, bonds, preferred stocks, debentures, and options—for the purpose of raising capital.

Most of the assignments for paralegals in this area relate to initial stock offerings; secondary stock, bond, or limited partnership offerings; private placement offerings; reporting requirements of securities trading; and the registration of securities with the state. But what a securities law paralegal does on a day-to-day basis depends on where he or she works. A paralegal in a law firm could work exclusively on initial stock offerings, while a paralegal in a corporation could spend the majority of the time preparing filings. Before listing some of the responsibilities a securities law paralegal might have, I thought some background on securities would be helpful.

A security is evidence of the right to participate in the profits of a business. There are two types of securities: equity, which represents an ownership interest, and debt, which represents a promise to pay. Securities are sold by individuals and corporations to raise capital. The most familiar kinds of securities are stocks and bonds, but there are others—including preferred stock, debentures, warrants, and options. A limited partnership interest in real estate or in an oil or gas venture is also considered a security.

Speculative trading in stocks and bonds in the 1920s led to an inflated securities market and, ultimately, to the financial crash of 1929. Five years later, in 1934, the Securities and Exchange Commission was created as a federal administrative agency to regulate and supervise the sale of securities. (Sales are also regulated by the state.) Two major federal statutes that regulate the area are the Securities Act of 1933 and the Securities Exchange Act of 1934. The 1933 act regulates the initial issuance of securities. It requires companies to disclose certain information so that investors can make informed investment decisions. The 1934 act regulates trading after the initial issuance. It was put in place to prevent fraud and manipulation in connection with the purchase and sale of securities. (Remember Ivan Boesky and the insider-trading scandals of the mid to late 1980s? The 1934 act was supposed to prevent illegal activities like these from happening.)

The state laws that regulate securities are called blue sky laws. The term comes from a 1917 Supreme Court decision that upheld the state laws by stating that the laws attempted to prevent "speculative schemes [that] have no more basis than so many feet of 'blue sky.'"

The following example will help you understand how these laws affect small businesses. Let's say that you start a computer software business in your home. After a year, you decide to incorporate. A few of your friends contribute $5,000 each and become shareholders. You also get a bank loan. After a while, it becomes apparent that you need to raise more money. Where do you get it? If the business is successful, you could try either a private placement (a stock offering to a limited number of people) or a public offering (a stock offering to the general public). A private placement would exempt you from certain registration requirements under the federal and state securities laws. However, it limits the number of investors who can purchase shares and the total dollar value of shares you can offer for sale. If your company meets certain financial requirements, you would qualify for an initial public offering and be free from the restrictions of a private placement. (In the early to mid 1980s, entrepreneurs, such as Steve Jobs of Apple Computer, became millionaires overnight by offering shares of their new companies to the public.)

Once your company goes public, it must comply with the reporting requirements of the Securities Exchange Act of 1934. The act requires filing various annual and quarterly reports and reports regarding the purchase or sale of stock by officers or directors, dividends, and proxy statements.

Some of the responsibilities a securities law paralegal might include:

- Drafting portions of the registration statement (a document that discloses the plans, objectives, and financial information of a company to potential purchasers of the company's securities)

- Preparing documents, such as questionnaires, for officers and directors, underwriting agreements, and preliminary blue sky memoranda

- Filing the registration statement and working with the financial printer

- Preparing applications to register securities in various states and other blue sky tasks

- Preparing reports under the Securities Exchange Act of 1934, including proxy statements, 10-K and 10-Q forms, annual reports to shareholders, stock exchange listing applications, and insider trading reports

- Assisting in preparation of private offering circulars

- Preparing for and attending private placement closings

As I stated at the beginning of this chapter, after a year of litigation work, I switched over to this field. I found it extremely interesting and challenging and recommend it to anyone who's interested in a long-term paralegal career.

Real Estate: A Primary Practice Area

Less than 15 percent of all paralegals work in real estate law. Real estate laws govern the ownership and transferability of real property. Real property refers to an interest in land or buildings as distinguished from personal property, which refers to any transportable good.

As a law practice area, real estate law involves one or more of the following activities: representation of the buyer or seller in commercial, residential, or industrial real estate purchases or sales; representation of the lender or borrower in real estate financings; representation of the landlord or tenant in leasehold matters; real estate litigation, if any; and the real estate aspects of corporate transactions.

Phases of a Real Estate Transaction

In a real estate transaction that involves the purchase, sale, or financing of property, there are four phases in which paralegals play an integral role. These are determining title, preparing for the closing, attending the closing, and the postclosing follow-up.

In the first phase, the primary concern is to determine the status of title to the property. Having title to something means having the right to possess it. Title to a property may be affected by certain rights, or encumbrances, upon the property by other individuals. One such right is called a lien, which is a claim upon the property as security for debt owed. A common type of lien is a mechanic's lien for the payment of money owed for labor, services, or material furnished in erecting or repairing a building on the property. (Many of the tasks performed by real estate paralegals center on the concept of title.)

In the second phase of a transaction, the paralegal's role is to coordinate all details to ensure a smooth closing. The tasks performed in this phase include drafting various closing documents, such as deeds, mortgages, bills of sale, promissory notes, and assignments of lease; estimating closing costs; and working with the title company in clearing any objections to the title report. The closing, the third phase, is an interesting and rewarding time for paralegals since it represents the culmination of hours of hard work. During the closing, the paralegal would manage all documents, obtain signatures, and work with the title company.

The final phase involves postclosing duties, which include preparation of a binder containing all closing documents and follow-up work with the title company.

— **Selected Real Estate Law Terminology** —

Abstract of title—A short history or record of the chain of title.

Assignment—Any transfer of one party's rights or interest in a property to another party.

Closing—In real property, the stage at which the buyer of real estate pays the money due under the contract in exchange for the deed to the property.

Easement—The right to use the land belonging to another; usually the right to use the land of a neighbor.

Encumbrance—Anything that may restrict a party's title to property, thereby potentially reducing its value.

Title policy—An insurance policy for the buyer of real property that guarantees that the title is marketable and insures the buyer against damages if some defect in the title is found at a later date.

Title search—An investigation of public records to trace the title rights to real property. The object is to trace the chain of title and determine whether or not the property can be passed to another party free and clear of encumbrances. The end product of a search is the abstract of title.

Unlawful detainer—A proceeding that gives landlords a means of gaining the possession of rental property from a tenant or that provides tenants with protection from forceful eviction. Known as dispossess or distress proceedings in some states.

Many of the tasks performed by paralegals in a real estate practice depend on whether the law firm represents the purchaser, seller, lender, or borrower. Other considerations are the type of property and the kind of transaction involved; these include single-family dwellings, condominiums, and industrial sites; commercial leases, partnerships, foreclosures, and financings; and landlord/tenant matters. Real estate paralegals who work on a purchase, sale, or financing could be responsible for:

- Conducting title searches and updates
- Preparing a preliminary abstract of title and an opinion on the title
- Assisting clients to obtain mortgage financing and to record mortgages
- Drafting, reviewing, and analyzing documents, such as truth-in-lending disclosure statements, easements, legal de-

scriptions of property, deeds, leases, assignments, escrow instructions, and closing statements

- Preparing formal lien clearances
- Obtaining documents that relate to a borrower's financial condition
- Conducting UCC searches
- Preparing for and attending closings
- Performing postclosing work, such as obtaining canceled notes, deeds of trust, or title policies, and assisting clients to obtain liability insurance

In a corporate legal department, real estate paralegals may assist in employee relocation. The paralegal can aid in the sale and/or purchase of a home by coordinating the activities of real estate brokers, title companies, and real estate lawyers. In addition, since a corporation must file property tax returns for each state in which it has property, paralegals may maintain property ownership records, analyze tax assessments, assist in drafting the company's response to tax adjustments, and monitor tax legislation that affects the property.

In a corporation or a firm, the paralegals who specialize in real estate law often perform tasks similar to those who work in corporate law or litigation. For instance, when preparing a closing for a corporate client, a real estate paralegal might draft shareholder or director resolutions, tasks that are also done by corporate paralegals. The litigation-type duties in real estate law involve mortgage foreclosures, unlawful detainer actions (landlord/tenant disputes), and actions that determine who owns title to property.

"I really enjoyed working in real estate and believe it's an important area for paralegals to specialize in," says Peggy Ruse about her experiences as a real estate paralegal in a large San Francisco law firm. "I worked very independently and was given a lot of responsibility. Some of my duties were drafting documents, negotiating title insurance with title companies, and preparing for real estate closings. I became an expert in title insurance and found that attorneys rely very heavily on paralegals in this area. I might caution paralegals interested in this area that real estate paralegals often work long hours—particularly when preparing for and attending closings. Basically, you don't go home until the deal is done." Peggy, who now works as a paralegal for Hewlett-Packard in Palo Alto, California, believes that real estate paralegals can advance into real estate development by working in commercial property sales and development.

I find it interesting that, in keeping with statistics on the low percentage of paralegals who work in real estate, Peggy was the only paralegal, of the dozens I randomly chose to interview for this book, who had experience working in real estate law.

Estate Planning/Probate: A Primary Practice Area

Less than 10 percent of all paralegals work in the two-part specialty field of estate planning and probate. Estate planning refers to the management and distribution of property, including wills, trusts, gifts, taxes, and investments. Probate is the legal process through which a court decides on the validity of a will, reviews its provisions, and orders the final disposition of the assets of the estate.

Estate Planning

The laws that govern the estate planning field deal with the disposition of real and personal property. Most people are familiar with the concept of a will—the traditional way of transferring property to heirs. A will is merely the declaration of a person's desires about how his or her property should be disposed of after death. Its purpose is to prevent the state from distributing the estate according to state laws. But there's more to estate planning than the preparation of a will. Other legal devices can be used to dispose of property or assets—among them trusts (property held by one person for the benefit of another) and outright gifts. These devices are not subject to probate procedures, which are often costly and time-consuming.

The responsibilities of a paralegal employed in an estate planning practice include:

- Analyzing client assets and financial information
- Preparing tax calculations
- Monitoring state statutes to ensure that estate plans conform to state law
- Drafting legal documents such as wills, trust agreements, and documents that relate to trust funds
- Preparing summaries of provisions of wills and trust agreements

- Recording asset transfer documents
- Completing trust registration and advising clients of notice requirements
- Obtaining, reviewing, and analyzing insurance policies
- Preparing change of beneficiary forms
- Updating wills to comply with changes in the laws

Selected Estate Planning/ ProbateTerminology

Accounting—In probate law, a court action, process, or formal investigation to determine the amount, status, and/or disposition of a deceased person's assets and liabilities, or those of his or her estate.

Probate—The process for establishing the validity of the document purported to be the will of a deceased person.

Trust—A property interest held by one party for the benefit of another.

Trustee—A person who holds property in trust for another (the beneficiary). The trustee has legal title to the property and the beneficiary has beneficial title to the property.

Probate

Several types of matters are filed in probate court, including estate proceedings (of which there are two types—*testate* proceedings, in which a person dies and leaves a will, and *intestate* proceedings, in which no will is left), *conservatorships* (in which a court appoints an individual to care for the property and/or person of someone determined to be unable to manage his or her own property), and *guardianships* (in which the court appoints an individual to care for the person and/or property of a minor).

The steps involved in a typical probate matter consist of holding the initial conference with the client or closest family member (if the client is deceased), commencing probate proceedings, taking inventory of the assets of the decedent's estate, valuating those assets, paying the decedent's debts and expenses, making an accounting to the court, filing tax returns (estate tax, inheritance tax, etc.), and, ultimately, distributing assets and closing the estate. In a probate proceeding, a paralegal's assignments might involve:

- Taking an inventory of the decedent's home
- Opening the safe deposit box for burial instructions and/or the will
- Locating witnesses to prove the authenticity of the will
- Corresponding with institutions to obtain asset information
- Obtaining copies of the death certificate
- Publishing the death notice in newspapers
- Preparing a petition for probate of the will
- Filing claims for insurance proceeds and death benefits
- Preparing disallowance of claims against the estate
- Itemizing and appraising the value of estate assets
- Preparing documents for the sale of assets
- Paying debts, liens, and expenses
- Preparing gift, estate, inheritance, and other tax returns
- Requesting a final audit
- Applying for release of estate assets
- Preparing final and supplemental accountings
- Transferring assets to heirs

Because the majority of tasks involve the preparation of tax returns, accountings, and asset valuations, probate paralegals must be fairly good with numbers. "For people who want to get into the probate area, I recommend an accounting class, as well as a class in investments," suggests Mary Beth Schultz, a probate, tax, and estates paralegal at Jensen, Hicken, Gedde & Scott in Anoka, Minnesota. "Also, a person should be detail oriented and enjoy working with numbers, since a lot of the work involves taxes and preparing final accountings for estates."

Other Legal Specialties

While most paralegals work in litigation, corporate, real estate, or estate planning/probate law, there are several other areas of law that provide employment opportunities for paralegals. These include bankruptcy, intellectual property, labor law, employee benefit plans, and workers' compensation.

Bankruptcy

These days, bankruptcy law is big business. For example, in 1987 there were over 561,000 bankruptcies filed in the United

States—a 100 percent increase over the 278,000 petitions filed just seven years earlier.

Bankruptcy is the legal process that, under federal law, gives a debtor a fresh start and ensures that his or her creditors are treated as fairly as possible. There are several forms of relief available under the federal bankruptcy laws. Those most commonly used are Chapter 7, which involves liquidating a person's assets; Chapter 11, which involves reorganizing a corporation; and Chapter 13, which involves adjusting a person's debts. To initiate bankruptcy proceedings, either a voluntary petition or an involuntary petition must be filed by the debtor or creditor, respectively, in bankruptcy court. Law firms that specialize in bankruptcy may act as a trustee or represent the debtor or the creditor in court proceedings.

Working for a trustee. Bankruptcy paralegals may be employed by lawyers or nonlawyers who act as the bankruptcy trustee. Once a bankruptcy is filed, the trustee is responsible for the recovery and liquidation of the debtor's assets and the payment of creditors' claims. Some of the paralegal's responsibilities include:

- Preparing demand letters to institutions and companies to notify them of the bankruptcy and request that they turn any of the debtor's funds over to the trustee
- Arranging for the appraisal of the debtor's assets
- Monitoring any transfer of assets or expenditure of funds during the bankruptcy proceedings
- Arranging for notice in newspapers concerning sale of the debtor's property
- Preparing a full accounting of the property sold
- Reviewing all claims before the distribution of funds to creditors

Working for a debtor. At a firm that represents a debtor, the paralegal's role would be to aid in the disclosure of information to interested parties about the debtor's financial situation; ensure that the debtor fulfills his or her obligations to creditors, the court, and the bankruptcy trustee; and, to the degree possible, preserve the debtor's assets. Some of the assignments would include:

- Gathering information and facts about the client's financial position
- Drafting the bankruptcy petition

- Arranging for UCC and real property searches
- Preparing a schedule of the debtor's assets and liabilities
- Listing claims for any property exempt under the bankruptcy code
- Preparing a statement of affairs
- Preparing for the first meeting of creditors
- Drafting and filing the debtor's monthly financial statements (in Chapter 11 cases)
- Drafting complaints in adversary proceedings
- Attending Chapter 13 plan confirmation hearings

Working for a creditor. The primary responsibility of a lawyer who represents a creditor is to protect and preserve the creditor's interests and obtain payment of his or her claim. Paralegals on this side of a bankruptcy case would be responsible for preparing and filing a formal proof of claim with the court. If the claim is secured by collateral—an interest in real or personal property— then the paralegal might assist in determining the status of the collateral, inspect the physical property, and review collateral documents such as mortgages and deeds.

One more thing: because bankruptcy proceedings place enormous financial and emotional burdens on the parties involved, paralegals who work in this area should be adept at handling sensitive personal issues.

Intellectual Property

As a practice area, intellectual property includes four broad categories: trademarks, patents, copyrights, and trade secrets. To understand the differences between the categories, you need only to refer to their respective bodies of law. Trademark law is concerned with protecting the exclusive right of merchants and manufacturers to use any name, word, symbol, or device to identify their goods and/or services. Patent law is concerned with protecting an inventor's exclusive right to make, use, or sell his or her invention over a specified period of time. Copyright law is concerned with protecting the exclusive right of writers and artists to publish their creative works and determining who may publish such works. Trade secrets law is concerned with protecting a business's exclusive right to use and keep secret from competitors any formula, pattern, machine, or manufacturing process that gives the business a competitive advantage.

Intellectual property is a highly specialized field. The area of patents, for instance, requires knowledge of technical and scientific terms. Very few paralegals work exclusively in the area of intellectual property. Unless you're hired by a very large corporation or a law firm that specializes in intellectual property, you're likely to work in other practice areas of law as well. During my year as a litigation paralegal, for instance, I also worked on assignments that dealt with the trademark registration of a popular ski resort in Lake Tahoe, Nevada.

Given the nature of the intellectual property practice, most paralegal tasks center on three types of activities: the search to ascertain the availability of trademarks and tradenames; registration with federal, state, and/or foreign agencies; and litigation at the administrative agency level (U.S. Patent and Trademark Office) and in the courts that involves trademark opposition or infringement matters.

The responsibilities of a paralegal who specializes in intellectual property law include:

- Conducting patent and trademark searches with computerized legal databases, such as LEXPAT
- Preparing patent and/or trademark status summary reports
- Drafting trademark and copyright registration applications
- Maintaining a calendar of due dates for renewals, responses, and oppositions and for payment of patent annuities in foreign countries
- Performing legal research regarding unfair competition matters
- Assisting in opposition, interference, and infringement proceedings
- Acting as liaison with foreign trademark/patent attorneys and agents
- Drafting license agreements regarding proprietary information and technology

Employee-Related Specialties

There are several legal practice areas directly related to employment issues, workers, and employees. Among them are labor law, employee benefit law, and workers' compensation.

Labor law. A labor law practice involves many different types of transactions, including collective bargaining, proceedings before the National Labor Relations Board (NLRB), arbitration, matters arising under federal and state wage and hour laws, Equal Employment Opportunity Commission (EEOC) investigations, discrimination cases, international labor matters, and litigation. The specific duties of a labor paralegal depend on whether he or she works in a law firm or corporation and who the client is (a union, an employee, or management). Obviously, good people skills are needed in this specialty. Paralegals often must deal with sensitive issues, such as representing management in an employee discrimination case.

A paralegal who works for a labor law practice would be responsible for:

- Collecting and analyzing data for collective bargaining negotiations
- Performing economic analyses of union proposals
- Preparing comparisons of labor/management settlements from similar industries and analyzing recent trends
- Attending bargaining sessions and taking notes
- Preparing first drafts of bargaining agreements
- Preparing for NLRB hearings
- Drafting petition letters to NLRB in defense of an unfair labor practice charge
- Preparing for trial (similar to civil litigation) when formal complaints are issued by the NLRB
- Preparing for arbitration proceedings
- Reviewing and analyzing documents that relate to complaints of noncompliance to minimum wage or overtime provisions of federal or state laws
- Preparing for EEOC investigations
- Reviewing and analyzing employers' affirmative action plans
- Preparing documents in EEO litigation matters

Employee benefit plans. The Employment Retirement Income Security Act of 1974 (ERISA) created new regulations to govern the qualification, disclosure, and reporting requirements of employee pension plans. In recent years, attorneys have turned more and more to paralegals to administer these regulations.

Paralegals should be familiar with several different types of employee benefit plans, including individual retirement accounts (IRAs), Keoghs, and profit-sharing, money purchase, deferred compensation, stock bonus, employee stock purchase, and stock option plans. Pension and profit-sharing plans may be either qualified, which allows an employer deduction and requires IRS approval, or unqualified, which does not require IRS approval and grants no deduction to the employer.

Paralegals who specialize in employee benefit plans would be responsible for:

- Drafting plans and reviewing existing plans
- Obtaining IRS approval of plans
- Filing applications for IRS determination letters
- Drafting plan summary descriptions
- Assisting in the preparation of reports and disclosure information, including annual reports to the IRS and summary plan descriptions to plan participants
- Drafting notification of participation, election to participate, beneficiary designation, and other election documents
- Drafting promissory notes and salary assignments for participant loans
- Answering employee inquiries (if working in a corporate setting)
- Determining valuation adjustments and making allocations to participants' accounts
- Calculating participants' years of service for vesting purposes
- Administering plans, including paying termination benefits and loan proceeds, tracking loan repayments, and filing IRS 1099 forms for payments made

One of the advantages of specializing in ERISA is that paralegals can easily transfer their skills to nonparalegal jobs in personnel or employee benefits departments. I know of one major San Francisco law firm that recently created a new title for ERISA paralegals—benefit specialist—which enables them to be paid more.

Workers' compensation. Recall from Chapter 3 that administrative law is one of the four levels of law that govern our society. It involves the decisions, regulations, and rulings of administrative agencies. One such agency is the Workers' Compensation Appeals Board (WCAB), an administrative agency that regulates the compensation of people who are injured on the job. The statutes that govern workers' compensation establish the employer's liability for an employee's injury or sickness arising from his or her work.

As with other administrative agencies, the WCAB allows nonlawyers to represent a client before it. As a result, paralegals who work in this specialty field have a wide range of responsibilities. In fact, a formal opinion issued in February 1989 by the state bar of California declared that paralegals may appear before the WCAB, provided the client approves. Since workers' compensation cases deal with personal injury matters, many of the duties involved are similar to those performed by litigation paralegals in tort cases. They include:

- Obtaining a copy of an accident report
- Drafting a request for hearing or response
- Obtaining medical authorizations, medical reports, and personnel information
- Scheduling physician appointments and independent medical exams
- Interviewing physicians, experts, and witnesses
- Preparing narrative case evaluations
- Evaluating disability and researching claims options
- Assisting in settlement negotiations
- Drafting documents such as a petition for review, the issue and fact section of an appellate brief, and a notice for reconsideration

Other Practice Areas

This chapter has presented the traditional areas of paralegal employment (including those in which you are most likely to find your first job!). But there are dozens of other fields of law that provide potential employment opportunities for paralegals, including aviation, communications, entertainment, food and drug law, hospital and health care, immigration, international trade, maritime and admiralty law, media, military law, natural resources (mining, oil, and gas), public benefits, sports, tax law, and transportation—to name a few.

As you have seen in this chapter and in Chapter 3, there are many tasks, such as conducting legal research, reading and summarizing documents, drafting documents, and monitoring laws and statutes, that are common to a number of legal specialty areas. There are also tasks that are specifically related to particular practice areas. The most important thing to remember, however, is that paralegal responsibilities vary greatly depending on the nature of the employer (corporation, law firm, or government agency), the attitude of the supervising attorney, and the paralegal's own skills, among other things. The combination of these factors makes each position unique.

Now that you have a general idea of just what it is that paralegals do, you can combine this knowledge with your own individual interests, skills, and experience to help you with your job search. Chapter 8 aids in this process by summarizing the advantages and disadvantages of each specialty area. The next chapter focuses on everyone's favorite topic: salary. Additional information on paralegal education and experience is also provided.

Chapter

5

How Much Do
Paralegals Earn?

Earn a little, and spend a little—less.

John Stevenson

While I was browsing through a legal journal one day, a headline caught my eye. It read:

"$100,000 A YEAR FOR PARALEGALS?
Texas Firm Expands Authority, Benefits for Nonlawyers"

Sound too good to be true? Well, for the most part it is, but several legal assistants in that one Texas law firm *do* earn that amount. According to one of the partners in the firm, "Three or four non-lawyers are paid far above the norm because they are worth it. We reward productivity wherever we find it." A rare employer indeed! Before you run to the nearest paralegal training program, stop and think. Nothing like that ever comes easy. A person with the title "paralegal" generally won't make $100,000 per year.

So, what *can* you expect to earn as a paralegal? Depending primarily on the area of the country you live in, entry-level paralegals start at $20,000 to $25,000 per year, paralegals with two to four years of experience can earn $25,000 to $35,000 per year, and paralegals with five or more years of experience generally earn $35,000 and above. More important, however, is the fact that people with paralegal skills and training can make far above those averages by parlaying their experience into other areas of employment—related to law or not. For instance, I know someone who was able to transform several years of experience at a law firm into a higher-paying job at a corporation. He went from being an ERISA paralegal to a pension administrator. His responsibilities didn't change, but his salary sure did.

The Problem with Titles

The ability to obtain a job title that accurately reflects the duties being performed (and, of course, being a specialist) is the key to obtaining a higher salary. Getting an employer to create a new title, however, isn't easy.

There are many occupations—such as those in teaching, medicine, and social work—that have standardized job descriptions that include salary ranges. But the paralegal profession is not among them. Why not? To begin with, there is very little standardization regarding educational requirements and on-the-job responsibilities. The tasks performed by paralegals continue to increase in scope and complexity, which makes it impossible to come up with a single standardized job description. Not having a standardized job description is a plus when it allows for a wide variety of responsibilities, but a minus when it comes to trying to peg a salary to a job by its title alone. For instance, the responsibilities of a first-year litigation paralegal who spends most of the day organizing documents are quite different from those of a fifth-year probate paralegal who is specialized and an expert in a particular area. Both have the title of paralegal; should they be paid the same? I hope not.

One solution would be for employers to create different titles for paralegals who become specialists in a particular practice area. After working for four years as a corporate paralegal, I received a call from the general counsel of a large San Francisco corporation who wanted to hire me as a paralegal for a newly created position. The job sounded interesting because it combined several areas, including shareholder relations, corporate communications, and computers, with regular paralegal and legal administration duties. I was interested in it, but I didn't feel the title paralegal adequately represented its responsibilities and believed it would limit the salary range. The general counsel agreed. I accepted the job and was given the title legal administrator, which put my salary in a higher range than I would have gotten as a paralegal.

Paralegal Profiles

The paralegal profession is a melting pot of diverse individuals whose educational and occupational backgrounds are quite varied. While it can be said that the average paralegal works in a law firm, possesses a bachelor's degree and/or a paralegal certificate, has four to six years of paralegal experience, and works in the area of litigation, there are many variations on that theme (as you'll see in the pages to come).

The following information on salary, education, experience, and training was compiled to help you determine whether a paralegal career is right for you. However, it is presented with a few caveats. The statistical information was gathered from surveys taken by various local and regional paralegal associations in 1988 or 1989, *if* such information was available. Many paralegal associations don't collect this kind of information, which means not all cities, states, and regions could be compared. Also, differences in the ways questions were posed on the surveys affect the ways they were answered and are marked on the charts by asterisks and noted accordingly. As such, the profiles presented in this chapter represent a general picture of what's going on in the profession in various areas of the country and are not intended to give a statistically precise comparison of paralegals across the nation.

Base Salary

Base salaries for paralegals in the cities, states, and regions surveyed range from $13,500 to over $80,000 per year. This huge difference is due to several factors, including geographic area, type of employer, size of employer, years of experience, and legal specialty area. It's also related to intangibles such as attorney attitude toward paralegals. Although paralegals have been a part of the legal profession for over two decades, not every employer understands what they are and how to use them. To some attorneys, paralegals are nothing more than document clerks, while others see them as highly skilled legal technicians who can perform a wide range of complex tasks.

The three major factors that affect paralegal salaries are years of experience, legal specialty area, and type of employer. The figures in the following charts represent base salary as a function of these factors and serve only as a guideline. They don't include bonuses, overtime, or other forms of compensation. Also, since the figures are from 1989 and 1988, you'll need to adjust them by adding 8–10 percent per year (the average annual salary increase for paralegals) to estimate salary levels for subsequent years.

Base Salary Ranges

Cities

Dallas	$14,000–80,000
Kansas City, Mo.	Less than $16,000–37,999
Los Angeles	$18,000–68,000
Philadelphia	$14,000–50,000+
St. Louis	Less than $20,000–44,999
San Francisco	$16,800–64,000

States

Georgia*	$5,400–50,400
Minnesota	Less than $14,000–45,000
Washington	$14,000–43,999

Regions

Rocky Mountain	$14,000–42,000
Washington, D.C.–	
Virginia–Maryland	$13,500–50,500

*Includes hourly and part-time wages.

Sources: Dallas Association of Legal Assistants 1989 Salary and Compensation Survey, Kansas City Association of Legal Assistants 1989 Employment Survey, Los Angeles Paralegal Association 1989 Employment and Salary Survey, Philadelphia Association of Paralegals 1989 Salary and Benefits Survey, St. Louis Association of Legal Assistants 1989 Annual Employment Survey, San Francisco Association of Legal Assistants 1989 Survey, Georgia Association of Legal Assistants 1989 Employment and Salary Survey, Minnesota Association of Legal Assistants 1988 Salary and Benefits Survey, Washington Legal Assistants Association 1988 Survey, Rocky Mountain Legal Assistants Association 1988 Survey, and National Capital Area Paralegal Association 1988 Salary Survey.

The figures from Dallas and San Francisco in the chart below seem to suggest that paralegals with over ten years in the field generally experience diminished returns in terms of salary.

Base Salary Ranges by Years of Experience

Experience	Washington, D.C.–Virginia–Maryland	Dallas	San Francisco
Less than 1 year	$13,500–26,000	$16,001–36,000	—
1–2 years	18,000–28,000	14,001–45,000	$16,800–45,000
3–4 years	22,000–36,000	18,001–80,000+	15,450–48,150
5–6 years	21,500–33,000	24,001–42,000	24,000–46,600
7–8 years	24,500–37,300	18,001–50,000	18,500–57,200
9–10 years	21,500–46,200	26,001–60,000	15,000–64,000
10+ years	27,000–50,500	24,001–50,000	20,250–56,400

Sources: National Capital Area Survey, Dallas Survey, and San Francisco Survey.

It's interesting to note that in the following chart, the highest-paying specialty area is different in each location.

Base Salary Ranges by Primary Specialty Area

Cities	Litigation	Corporate
Dallas	$14,001–55,000	$20,001–50,000
San Francisco	15,000–64,000	16,800–54,000
States		
Georgia*	14,400–44,000	18,000–50,000
Washington	14,000–35,999	18,000–39,999

Cities	Real Estate	Estate Planning/ Probate
Dallas	18,001–60,000	16,001–42,000
San Francisco	18,600–51,264	21,600–56,400
States		
Georgia*	5,400–40,870	6,480–37,500
Washington	22,000–43,999	22,000–39,999

*Includes hourly and part-time wages.

Sources: Dallas Survey, San Francisco Survey, Georgia Survey, and Washington Survey.

The chart below presents average salaries, reported by the National Capital Area Paralegal Association's 1988 Salary Survey, as a means to compare salaries in the four primary practice areas with those in other specialty areas.

Average Salary by Practice Area*

Primary areas	Average 1988 salaries
Litigation	$26,815
Corporate	26,586
Real Estate	29,400
Estate Planning/Probate	28,767
Other	
Banking	19,833
Environmental	22,625
Bankruptcy	24,350
Trademark	27,250
ERISA	30,138
Blue Sky/Securities	31,333
Tax	32,833
Government Contracts	33,550

*Washington, D.C.–Virginia–Maryland.

Base Salary Ranges by Employer

Location	Law Firm
Washington, D.C.–Virginia–Maryland	
0–25 attorneys	$13,500–46,200
26–50 attorneys	18,000–40,000
51–100 attorneys	19,500–36,000
Over 100 attorneys	19,500–50,500
Georgia*	
1–10 attorneys	11,000–35,600
11–50 attorneys	20,000–32,300
51–100 attorneys	18,000–35,339
Over 100 attorneys	5,400–44,000
San Francisco	
1–9 attorneys	16,200–41,520
10–39 attorneys	15,000–45,000
40–99 attorneys	18,500–63,000
100+ attorneys	15,450–64,000

Location	Corporation	Government Agency
Washington, D.C.–Virginia–Maryland	$22,000–35,000	$23,907–39,860
Georgia*	18,000–50,000	21,504–29,700
San Francisco	23,616–49,800	20,000–36,000

*Includes hourly and part–time wages.

Sources: National Capital Area Survey, Georgia Survey, and San Francisco Survey. The Georgia Survey also reported salary ranges for other employers, including nonprofit organizations ($23,000–29,000) and banks ($19,500–28,000).

In addition to base salary, compensation often includes bonuses and, less often, overtime pay. Not all paralegals receive bonuses or overtime pay, but many do, and it significantly increases their annual compensation. Some surveys indicate that bonuses range from $100 to $20,000 per year. No statistics on the range of overtime paid out were available.

Education and Training

Individuals who enter the paralegal field bring with them a wide variety of educational backgrounds, including bachelor's and master's degrees in social science, legal studies, geology, environmental science, international relations, political science, architecture, English, history, music, accounting, finance, German, and elementary education—to name a few. As the chart below indicates, most paralegals hold a bachelor's degree and a paralegal certificate.

Education and Training

Location	% with high school/ no college	% with some college/ no degree	% with associate degree
Cities			
Dallas	–	21	14
Kansas City, Mo.	4	38	–
Los Angeles	1	15	11
Philadelphia	4	10	10
San Francisco	–	16	7
States			
Georgia	3	11	5
Minnesota	–	12	20
Washington	4	14	15
Regions			
Rocky Mountain	3	18	8
Washington, D.C.–			
Virginia–Maryland	10	–	13

Location	% with bachelor's degree	% with graduate studies*	% with paralegal certificate
Cities			
Dallas	55	7	69
Kansas City, Mo.	51	7	70
Los Angeles	65	10	80
Philadelphia	74**	–	79
San Francisco	77	25	45
States			
Georgia	67	13	–
Minnesota	60	–	72
Washington	55	6	45
Regions			
Rocky Mountain	63	8	63
Washington, D.C.–			
Virginia–Maryland	62	15	71

*Includes graduate course work, master's, doctorates, and J.D.'s.
**Includes bachelor's and master's degrees.

Sources: Dallas Survey, Kansas City Survey, Los Angeles Survey, Philadelphia Survey, San Francisco Survey, Georgia Survey, Minnesota Survey, Washington Survey, Rocky Mountain Survey, and National Capital Area Survey.

Years of Experience

As the paralegal profession matures, a large number of paralegals are remaining in the field. The following is a breakdown of working paralegals by the number of years of experience they have, as reported by the Minnesota Association of Legal Assistants 1988 Salary and Benefits Survey. These results, which show that the majority of paralegals responding to the survey have four to six years of experience, are reflective of the results of surveys from around the country.

Years of Experience

Experience	Percent of paralegals in the work force
Less than 1 year	14
1–3 years	26
4–6 years	30
7–10 years	21
11–16 years	7
Over 16 years	1

Type of Employer

The following chart presents a breakdown of whom paralegals work for.

Type of Employer

Location	Law Firm	Corporation	Government Agency
Cities			
Los Angeles	79%	11%	2%
Philadelphia	82	12	1
St. Louis	65	27	6
State			
Georgia	76	18	2
Region			
Rocky Mountain	83	8	7

Location	Self-Employed	Other*	Nonprofit
Cities			
Los Angeles	7%	2%	–
Philadelphia	1	5	–
St. Louis	2	–	–
State			
Georgia	–	3	1%
Region			
Rocky Mountain	2	–	–

*Includes banks, litigation support companies, consulting firms, and paralegal companies.

Sources: Los Angeles Survey, Philadelphia Survey, St. Louis Survey, Georgia Survey, and Rocky Mountain Survey.

Areas of Specialization

As stated in Chapter 3, more than 50 percent of all paralegals work in litigation. Since litigation is the meat and potatoes of most law firms, it's a great area in which to begin a career, but there are dozens of other specialty areas that employ paralegals, including the three other primary areas: corporate, real estate, and estate planning/probate. Landing a job in any of these areas just takes more effort than landing one in litigation. The chart below shows the percentage of paralegals who work in these practice areas.

Areas of Specialization*

Location	Litigation	Corporate	Real Estate	Estate Planning/ Probate
Cities				
Kansas City, Mo.	46%	14%	7%	9%
Philadelphia	36	11	9	10
San Francisco	65	19	8	8
State				
Georgia	48	14	14	3
Region				
Rocky Mountain	64	22	25	11

*More than one answer possible.

Sources: Kansas City Survey, Philadelphia Survey, San Francisco Survey, Georgia Survey, and Rocky Mountain Survey.

Other specialty areas that employ between 5 percent and 25 percent of all paralegals include banking, bankruptcy, family law, personal injury, securities, and workers' compensation. The specialty areas that employ less than 5 percent of paralegals include administrative law, criminal law, employee benefits, finance, intellectual property, labor law, legislative law, and tax law.

Billable Hours and Rates

Of course, this category applies only to paralegals who work in law firms, since corporations and government agencies don't require paralegals to bill their hours. With law firms becoming more cost conscious, more firms than ever before require their paralegals to bill a minimum number of hours per year.

According to these surveys, billable hours range from a low of 200 hours per year (St. Louis) to a high of 2,220 hours (Washington, D.C.–Virginia–Maryland). The San Francisco and Washington State surveys reported 1,551 and 1,468, respectively, as the average number of billable hours. Billing rates vary widely and are tied in to practice areas. For instance, in Washington, D.C., litigation paralegals bill at $25 per hour while blue sky/corporate paralegals bill at $100 per hour. The average rate for most areas of the country was $50–$60 per hour.

Computer Use

Computers are becoming an integral part of the paralegal's day-to-day responsibilities. Some of the computer applications used by paralegals are word processing, calendaring, litigation support, timekeeping/billing, corporate maintenance, financial and tax analysis, database management, and case management. In the San Francisco Association of Legal Assistants 1989 Survey, 84 percent of all respondents used computers in their jobs. The following is a breakdown of computer use by paralegals as reported by the Rocky Mountain Legal Assistants Association 1988 Survey.

Computer Use*

Task	Percent of paralegals who use computers for these tasks
Word processing	34
Litigation support	28
Other**	16
Calendaring***	13
Timekeeping/billing	11
Conflict checks	3

*Rocky Mountain.
**Includes corporate maintenance, financial and tax analysis, database management, and case management.
***Also referred to as docketing.

Self-Employed Paralegals

As the paralegal profession matures, an increasing number of paralegals are striking out on their own. These include free-lance paralegals who work under the supervision of attorneys, as well as independent paralegals who offer services directly to the public. There's not much information available about independent paralegals, however, since in most states their services are considered unauthorized practice of law.

According to the Los Angeles Paralegal Association 1988 Salary Survey, which had the most comprehensive information on self-employed paralegals, 7 percent of all paralegals in L.A. were self-employed. According to the Los Angeles data, 45 percent of the self-employed paralegals worked in litigation, 42 percent in probate, 7 percent in corporate, and 7 percent in other areas. The average self-employed paralegal had a total of ten years of experience and had worked for four years before becoming self-employed. Gross income ranged from $1,000 to $90,000; the average gross income was $42,600. Net income ranged from $11,500 to $52,000; the average net income was $27,000. Most self-employed paralegals held a bachelor's or associate degree and a certificate from an ABA-approved program. They worked with eleven clients and handled thirty-three cases per year on average. Billable rates ranged from $18 to $100 per hour; the average was $40 per hour.

Methods of Obtaining Jobs

While it's not surprising that personal contacts seem to be the best way to find employment, other ways do work. (The use of classified ads as a means to find available jobs is discussed in more detail in Chapter 8.)

Methods of Obtaining Paralegal Employment

Method	Georgia	Minnesota	Dallas
Personal contacts	41%	–	–
School placement	17	8%	1%
Classified ad	14	24	10
Unsolicited resume	14	10	15
Promotion	8	20	13
Employment agency	4	10	12
Paralegal association/ networking	2	7	9
Knew someone within firm	–	12	22
Attorney referral	–	6	8
Other	–	7	7

Sources: Georgia Survey, Minnesota Survey, and Dallas Survey.

Job Satisfaction

Paralegal job satisfaction depends on a variety of factors, the most important of which are legal specialty area, type of employer, and the employer's attitude toward paralegals.

—————— Paralegal Job Satisfaction ——————

Satisfaction level	Minnesota	Dallas	Los Angeles
High	23%	37%	23%
Above average	45	37	47
Average	24	21	21
Below average	5	3	8
Low	2	2	2

Sources: Minnesota Survey, Dallas Survey, and Los Angeles Survey.

The results of the preceding surveys are in keeping with other, more comprehensive studies that indicate that paralegals are relatively well paid and satisfied with their jobs. To summarize what you've just read, compensation for paralegals varies depending on their location, the kind of organization they work for, their level of education, and their years of experience, among other things. Many paralegals receive bonuses and/or overtime pay in addition to their salary, but some don't. The surveys also indicate that the majority of paralegals hold a bachelor's degree and a paralegal certificate, work in litigation, and have between four and six years of experience. In addition, the surveys show that most paralegals obtain jobs through personal contacts, classified advertising, and school placement. It's important to remember, however, that the surveys also suggest *many* variations on these themes.

So far, this book has looked at who paralegals are, where they work, what they do, and how much they earn. The next chapter examines another vital issue—how to become a paralegal—and addresses educational and training alternatives and the skills that are needed for a successful career.

Chapter

6

How Do You Become a Paralegal?
Skills, Education, and Training

The roots of education are bitter, but the fruit is sweet.

Aristotle

It's your first day on the job. You're a newly minted paralegal armed with a certificate from an ABA-approved paralegal program. You also have a bachelor's degree in something interesting, but not too practical, such as English literature or philosophy. An associate, looking ragged and hurried, calls you into her office, mutters something about a partnership agreement, and barks an assignment at you that sounds pretty vague and incomprehensible. You don't want to appear stupid and ask questions, so you sit there and nod as if you know exactly what she is talking about. It's over in about a minute and a half, but the experience leaves you confused and panicky.

Lawyers are notorious for giving sketchy assignments with very little explanation and then disappearing for days only to reappear 10 minutes before the assignment is due. Believe it or not, oftentimes lawyers don't know exactly what they want. You could be given an assignment that gets changed five times before they figure out what they're after! This chapter gives you insight into the kinds of skills, education, and formal training you'll need to help you to cope with these and other attorney foibles and to perform your job tasks with confidence.

What You Need

Since the scenario mentioned above has occurred so often in my own experiences as a paralegal, I have come to identify three abilities that are essential to success in the field: the ability to locate resources, the ability to write, and common sense. I can't stress enough how important these are, and I guarantee that you'll rely on them daily.

The ability to locate resources and access information is extremely crucial for paralegals—as it is for people in many other occupations—as we move toward the twenty-first century. Lawyers are always in a hurry and always under pressure, and they generally want everything done yesterday. You need to know where to go for information if you're given a vague assignment and no one is available to answer your questions. The source could be a law library, a computer database file, a state regulatory agency, or any of the hundreds of other sources of data that exist.

Writing is the meat and potatoes of most paralegal assignments. If you like to write, this is a viable career option. One of the first things I learned as a paralegal is to put *everything* into writing, no matter how small or seemingly insignificant it was. In fact, a "memorandum to file" probably is a paralegal's best friend. The reason? Three years from now, when you're no longer working on the case, someone else may have to reconstruct it from your memoranda. The more clearly you document the things in it, the easier it will be to reconstruct. (Incidentally, memos to file are also great for proving that you actually performed a specific task as requested.)

One more thing: Strange as it may seem, most legal assignments require 10 percent ability and knowledge and 90 percent common sense.

Tools of the Trade

The skills you need for success with the day-to-day tasks and responsibilities of a paralegal can be broken down into three major groups.

- *Organizational skills.* The ability to stay on top of details; to manage, retrieve, and organize documents; and to administrate, coordinate, and schedule.
- *Communication skills.* The ability to get ideas across verbally and in writing (including legal writing, interpersonal relations, negotiating, investigating, interviewing, and supervising).

- *Analytical skills.* The ability to conduct legal, factual, statistical, and legislative research; to reason; to extract and utilize information; to interpret and apply laws and regulations; and to analyze and summarize facts and documents.

Most tasks performed by paralegals use all of these skill groups in some combination. For instance, I was once given an assignment to analyze and evaluate the defendants' responses to all of the plaintiff's requests for the production of documents and interrogatories to make sure that the defendants had, in fact, produced all the documents they said they had. I was also asked to make recommendations about additional documents to request from the defendants based upon my knowledge of the case.

Successful completion of the assignment depended on using each of the three skill areas in the following manner: *organizational*—locating and retrieving specific documents; *analytical*—extracting and interpreting information in the defendants' responses in relation to what was requested; and *communication*—writing a detailed memorandum to the partner on the case.

Of these skill groups, many experts now consider communication to be the one most vital to success as a paralegal. Dr. Molly Moore, assistant professor of business education at Minnesota's Moorhead State University, conducted an in-depth study to determine what communication skills are needed by legal assistants. Out of a list of seventy, the following were among the skills given a very high need rating by over 50 percent of the paralegals who participated.

- Correct use of written grammar
- Accurate spelling
- Correct use of punctuation
- Clear sentence construction
- Correct use of spoken grammar
- Clear expression of ideas
- Clear expression of instructions
- Tactful expression of unpleasant information
- Good telephone etiquette

Writing Skills. If I had to choose one particular skill as the most important, it would be writing. Not legal writing, mind you, just plain old writing. What's the difference? The first is meant to intimidate you. The second is meant to enlighten you.

One of the reasons people are so put off by lawyers is legalese—the language they use. As such, legal writing is often filled with confusing (some would say unnecessary, redundant, vague, and meaningless) words and phrases.

"Good legal writing should not differ, without good reason, from ordinary, well-written English," says Richard Wydick, law school professor at the University of California, Davis. Professor Wydick's book, *Plain English for Lawyers*, is one of the bestselling books for the field ever written. It was instrumental in promoting what is known as the "plain-language" movement in law that began in the mid-1970s.

Plain English for Lawyers contains the following chapters, the titles of which offer sound advice about good writing: "Omit Surplus Words," "Use Base Verbs, Not Nominalizations," "Prefer the Active Voice," "Use Short Sentences," "Arrange Your Words with Care," "Use Familiar, Concrete Words," and "Avoid Language Quirks."

- *Other skills.* The ability to use computers, to make decisions, to solve problems, to prioritize assignments, and to work independently with minimal supervision.

Prioritizing assignments without panicking and working with minimal supervision are elemental to on-the-job success. Working at a law firm requires handling many different cases and clients at once. For example, you're in the middle of drafting a legal research memorandum for one attorney—due the next day—when suddenly another attorney rushes into your office and hands you an assignment that needs to be done before the end of the day. Next, a client calls and asks you to send out the stock certificates that you promised would be ready three days ago. And then, almost at the same moment, your paralegal supervisor phones to ask for your help on a rush project for the real estate department. You must be able to determine the relative importance of each of these assignments and the most efficient and effective order for carrying them out.

This scenario is more likely to occur in a law firm than in a corporate legal department. As was discussed in Chapter 2, paralegals in a corporate legal department work for one client—the corporation—so there are usually fewer fires to put out than at a law firm, where multiple clients generally want things done "now." Prioritizing is essential.

Regarding supervision, attorneys are usually too busy to hover over you and monitor everything you do. This is great once you're experienced and know what you're doing, but it can be a bit nerve-racking for new paralegals who may have no clue about how to proceed on their own. Be patient—you may find the opportunity to work independently one of the pluses of the career.

Getting into Training

Because standardized educational requirements have not been accepted by the profession industry-wide and because employers use their own criteria when hiring paralegals, entry into the field is open to people with a wide range of experience. Although it is possible to land a position that provides on-the-job training or to become a paralegal via promotion, current trends indicate that people with some formal education or training—be that a bachelor's degree, a paralegal certificate, or an associate degree in paralegal studies—tend to be hired.

The Evolution of Paralegal Education

Before the various types of paralegal programs available today are discussed, a brief look at the history of paralegal education and training will help give you perspective.

Education and training for paralegals have evolved steadily over the last twenty years, much like the profession itself. Before formal programs were established in the early 1970s, most training took place on the job. The advent of certificate-granting programs signaled the growing acceptance within the legal profession of "paralegal" as a new career niche. And in 1972, the career gained further legitimacy when the ABA's Special Committee on Lay Assistants developed guidelines to evaluate and thus accredit paralegal training programs. The number of formal training programs nationwide grew from a few dozen to several hundred between 1972 and 1977.

Despite the proliferation of these programs, paralegals, as such, were still relatively unknown to many prospective employers. The 1970s saw most paralegal functions performed by legal secretaries and people trained in other fields.

Therese Cannon, dean of the School of Paralegal Studies at the University of West Los Angeles, recalls the emergence of the paralegal profession. "When I started out as placement director in 1974, almost no one in Los Angeles knew what a paralegal was. There were almost no jobs for paralegals. Almost all of the lawyers who contacted the school wanted a smart legal secretary who could operate independently. For the next six or seven years we had to do a tremendous amount of promotional work. Both UCLA and our school were instrumental in building the paralegal field here. It all changed around 1980, and during the last five years the number of job openings in Los Angeles has expanded dramatically."

By the mid-1980s, employers had begun to recognize formal paralegal education as a measure of competence in the field. Over 70 percent of the working paralegals who responded to a 1988 survey conducted by the NFPA indicated that they had received formal training compared to 30 percent in 1982.

Formal Training and Education

Today, over 30,000 students are enrolled in the more than 500 institutions nationwide that provide formal paralegal training. The institutions may be two-year colleges (which provide 40 percent of the programs), four-year universities and colleges, technical schools, and proprietary schools, and their programs may lead to a certificate, an associate degree, or a bachelor's degree.

Certificate programs. Certificate programs are the most prevalent type of paralegal training and are offered by two-year and four-year colleges, technical schools, and proprietary schools. For the most part, these programs provide only legal training, although some do include general education courses. They can take anywhere from three months (if attended full-time) to over two years to complete and are recommended for individuals who possess a bachelor's degree, have completed 30–60 units of college credit, or have some work experience.

To some, the major drawback of certificate programs is that they provide only a cursory pass of the material—their short time frame makes it impossible to cover subjects in detail. Observes Lyla Hines, senior paralegal at Baker, Mills & Glast in Dallas and formerly a paralegal program instructor, "I think that in some instances they try to shove too much information into the students without sufficient background. I understand the desire to have successful programs, but you can't take someone who has no legal background and expect them to learn torts and contracts as well as the practical aspects of working in a law office all in a 30-hour course."

Generally, certificate programs aren't recommended for recent high school graduates who have had little or no professional work experience. For people who have experience in the work force and want to change careers, however, these programs are ideal.

Below are examples of the curricula of two ABA-approved certificate programs.

The University of West Los Angeles offers a program leading to a legal assistant certificate. It is designed both for individuals with three or more years of work experience and for those who have completed 15 or more units of college-level work, and it doesn't require a bachelor's degree. The program can be completed on a part-time basis in two to three years.

In the 1989–90 school year, the following courses were required: Legal Theory and Practice, Principles of Accounting, Property, Torts, Contracts, Directed Research and Writing A, Directed Research and Writing B, and Litigation Specialization. The general electives were Understanding the Use of Computers in the Law Firm; Law Office Administration; Wills, Trusts, and Estate Planning; Family Law; Workers' Compensation; Bankruptcy Law and Procedure; Entertainment Law; Criminal Practice; and Immigration Practice. The electives offered in specialty areas were Probate Administration Specialization, Corporations Specialization, and Real Estate Specialization. The program also included 15 units of general education.

The second example is the curriculum from the Philadelphia Institute (formerly the Institute for Paralegal Training), a highly respected proprietary school. Specifically designed for individuals who have a bachelor's degree, in 1989 this program allowed students to specialize in administrative and public law, corporate finance and business law, employee benefit plans, fiduciary management, international trade law and business, litigation management, or real estate law or to study general practice.

While the specialty programs consisted of sixteen weeks of area-specific courses, the general practice program (also sixteen weeks) consisted of the following courses: Introduction to the Law and the Litigation Process, Introduction to Research, Computer Literacy for Paralegals, Personal Injury Law, Introduction to Criminal Law, Introduction to Corporate Law, Introduction to Commercial Law, Introduction to Real Estate, Family Law, and Estate Planning and Probate.

Associate degree programs. Some community and junior colleges and four-year universities and colleges offer two-year associate degrees in paralegal studies. Admission requirements for these programs include a high school diploma and, possibly, college-level aptitude test scores, writing samples, letters of recommendation, and personal interviews.

The curriculum usually is a combination of general education requirements, core legal courses (in research, writing, law office management, and an introduction to the field), business law, civil procedure, and legal specialty courses.

These programs are recommended for high school graduates with little or no professional work experience. An associate degree in paralegal studies can be used to land a job as a paralegal or as credit toward obtaining a bachelor's degree. (The second option is the major benefit and attraction of an associate degree.)

Kirkwood Community College in Cedar Rapids, Iowa, offers an ABA-approved program that leads to an associate degree in arts or science. Both degrees required general education courses and the following core requirements in the 1988–89 school year: Paralegal Orientation, Legal Ethics, Civil Litigation, Contracts/Torts, Legal Research/Writing, and a Legal Assistant Internship.

The associate degree in science additionally required 8 credit hours from the following electives: Criminal Procedural Law, Real Estate, Estate Planning/Administration, Business Organization, Family Law, Bankruptcy, Administrative Law, Income Tax, Criminal Law, and Constitutional Law.

Bachelor's degree programs. A small number of universities and colleges offer majors or minors in paralegal studies in their four-year degree programs. Although many of these were initiated in the early to mid 1970s, they are not as well-known as sources for paralegal training as certificate programs.

The curriculum requirements of these programs usually include general education and business courses as well as legal specialty courses. The programs combine both a generalist's and specialist's approach to the paralegal field. Many also offer internships in the senior year, which provide students with the opportunity to integrate classroom learning and on-the-job experience.

The major benefit of a bachelor's degree program is that it provides the student with a liberal arts background and skills that are immediately transferable to the workplace. Also, since the programs take four years to complete, each subject can be covered in depth. For instance, a legal writing and research course in a four-year program may take two semesters to complete, while the same material in a three-month certificate program may be covered in one month or less.

This kind of program is recommended for high school graduates who are planning on obtaining a degree from a four-year college. Jill E. Martin, attorney, professor, and chair of the legal studies department at Connecticut's Quinnipiac College, suggests that four-year programs provide recent high school graduates with the opportunity to attain the maturity needed for a job as a paralegal in a law firm, particularly when the program includes an internship and courses in law office management. She believes that certificate programs may be more suitable for older students who have had some college and work experience.

Quinnipiac's legal studies major is not a prelaw program. The curriculum for a bachelor's degree consists of a combination of liberal arts and business courses and thirteen legal studies courses. The following legal studies courses were required in the 1988–89 school year: Proseminar (Introduction to the Paralegal Career), Introduction to the American Legal System, Library Methods in the Law, Civil Procedure I, Civil Procedure II, Legal Writing, Law Office Management, Legal Internship I, and Legal Internship II. (Students are also required to complete a basic accounting course and a course in computer literacy.) Electives could be chosen from Criminal Justice; Business Entities; Administrative Agencies; Law and Older Persons; Family Law; Wills, Probate, and Estate Administration; and Land Transfer and Closing Procedures.

Making a Choice

As you have seen, there are several kinds of formal paralegal training programs available today. Paralegal education is big business, and new schools are opening their doors every day. Listed below are things you should consider when deciding on the program that is best for you.

ABA approval. For many employers, an ABA-approved program signifies quality. Out of the 500 formal programs that operate today, only 23 percent are ABA approved. Earning approval means a program meets strict guidelines regarding the number of semester hours and types of courses required for certification or a degree. The approval process also includes a review of a school's faculty, admission requirements, administrative staff, and job placement service.

Admission requirements. Admission requirements vary widely and depend on the type of certification that's offered. A certificate program generally requires either (1) a bachelor's degree or (2) work experience and/or one to two years of college. Programs that offer either a two-year or four-year degree require a high school diploma and may also require work experience, aptitude or achievement test scores, and demonstrated writing ability.

Length of study. The length of time required to complete a paralegal training or education program varies from three months to four years—depending on the type. (Keep in mind that most three-month programs require a bachelor's degree for admission.) Many programs offer full-time and part-time options with both day and evening classes.

Curricula. Most programs use a combination of two basic curriculum models—general, broad-based legal training and intensified training in legal specialty areas. General legal courses usually include an introduction to the paralegal profession, civil procedure, criminal law, legal research and writing, law office management, and, possibly, computer literacy. Legal specialty courses include real estate, probate, corporate/business, tax, criminal, and family law; estate planning; and litigation. All programs should offer courses in theory as well as practical skills.

Faculty composition. The qualifications of the people teaching the course work are just as important as the material that is covered. Instructors are usually attorneys, working paralegals, business executives, and specialists with expertise in a particular field (such as computers). The selection of instructors depends on factors such as teaching ability, work experience, expertise, and experience with paralegals in the workplace.

Placement services. Reputable programs provide job placement services for current students and alumni. These services should include opportunities for internships. (As Chapter 8 reveals, internships are a great way to obtain your first paralegal position while learning valuable on-the-job skills.)

Computer facilities. All programs do not offer computer training courses. Due to the increased demand for computer-literate paralegals, however, it's a good idea to consider only programs that have such training.

Enrollment. Class size generally should not exceed thirty-five students. Remember, the smaller the class, the more individual attention you'll receive and the better student participation and interaction will likely be.

Cost. When looking for the program that's right for you, don't be fooled by the notion that the more one costs, the better it is—that's not always true. Costs vary widely. In the San Francisco

Bay Area, for example, the cost of obtaining a paralegal certificate ranged from $150 to $6,450 in 1988. And across the country, some proprietary schools that have emerged in recent years are clearly out to make a buck. Look hard at what a particular school offers and what it costs; compare it to other schools.

Before you decide on a particular program, it's important to evaluate not only the program itself but your own situation. Are you a high school graduate with no experience? Are you returning to the work force after raising a family? Do you want to change careers? Do you have the time to pursue a program for two or three years? The paralegal field is open to a wide variety of individuals with different educational and work backgrounds, and there are a variety of programs to accommodate those needs. Not every program is right for you.

One word of warning: Ever since the U.S. Department of Labor released statistics on the paralegal profession in 1987, a whole new crop of paralegal programs and schools have sprung up. Some are good, others aren't. Be wary of the ones that are not ABA approved, charge a lot of money, and promise that you'll make $30,000 to start as an entry-level paralegal. Some of these programs are just cashing in on the federal statistics and have targeted paralegal education mainly as a way to fatten their wallets. Be a cautious consumer and get the facts *before* you invest your time and money in what could be a less than reputable program.

Laurie Roselle, paralegal coordinator at Rogers & Wells in New York City, has some sound advice: "Don't jump into a program. Don't take the word of the program director that the school is the best thing since sliced bread, because, of course, that's what they are going to say. Talk to former students. Call paralegal associations. Conduct your own research."

Do you really need that piece of paper? Only 28 percent of the paralegals who responded to the 1988 NFPA survey had not had formal training. The availability of paralegal training programs and their widespread acceptance by employers are making it increasingly difficult to land a job as a paralegal—particularly in a large law firm—without any formal training. That's not to say that it's impossible to obtain a job without it. It's been the practice of small law firms to promote legal secretaries to paralegals or to hire people without a paralegal certificate and train them on the job. But be forewarned—this is changing. For the most part, the days when you can walk in and be hired as a paralegal without any formal training are over.

Informal Training

Whatever program you choose, formal training and education are only one component of becoming a paralegal. They provide the foundation of knowledge but not the day-to-day skills you need for success. As in any profession, these important skills must be learned on the job.

Anyone who's in the work force will tell you that there's no substitute for on-the-job training. It's difficult to simulate in a classroom the real situations working paralegals face. Unfortunately, on-the-job training means anything from formal, in-house training programs to the take-the-ball-and-run approach. I have experienced both and will take formal, in-house training any day.

In-house training. Many law firms provide newly hired paralegals with in-house training and orientation programs. These programs introduce newcomers to the profession to basic legal concepts; specific tasks, such as summarizing depositions; computer systems; and management techniques. Programs are administered by a paralegal manager, an attorney, or a combination of both. The most successful programs have the support of the firm's partners, associates, and management.

Training often employs the use of "systems" binders for instruction in the procedures of a specific legal task, such as preparing a will. A binder will contain:

- Written step-by-step procedures
- Standardized forms
- Checklists
- Source materials
- Sample form letters
- Information regarding preparation of documents
- Master information containing basic data on a particular case

In addition to the systems binder, training may also include assignments based on hypothetical problems that are critiqued by the paralegal manager upon completion. Typically, new paralegals are also trained in legal research and writing and the use of LEXIS or WESTLAW and the law library.

Obviously, the larger the firm, the more resources it will have to devote to training programs. Paralegals hired by small firms and by corporations with small legal departments usually don't have the luxury of in-house programs. Those are the firms that generally hand off the ball and want you to run.

Susan Peifer, paralegal coordinator at Gordon & Rees in San Francisco, uses another approach to training that's been quite successful. "The entry-level paralegals are put through a training program that lasts one week. We teach them what to look for during discovery, how to summarize depositions, do a document production, use the law library, cite check, Shepardize, and Bates stamp. However, initially they aren't allowed to do these things on their own. [Training is followed by] a buddy, or mentor, system where they're assigned to a senior paralegal. [The buddy system] works well because the junior paralegal is learning while the senior paralegal is teaching."

Continuing Education

While continuing education applies to working paralegals who want to stay abreast of the trends and developments in the field, it's important to understand that continuing education should be an integral part of all paralegal careers. It is the supplement to both formal and informal education and training that helps paralegals keep up with the ever-changing laws and regulations in their particular specialty.

The San Francisco Association of Legal Assistants' 1988 survey reported that over 80 percent of the paralegals who responded received reimbursement for continuing education seminars and courses. These programs are offered through paralegal and bar associations as well as proprietary paralegal schools.

CLA Designation

Continuing education may also be used to maintain designation as a certified legal assistant (CLA). The CLA designation is bestowed by the National Association of Legal Assistants (NALA) as professional recognition of paralegals who have achieved and maintain a particular level of competence in the field. It is *not* the same as a paralegal certificate, which is awarded by an educational institution. The CLA designation is awarded by NALA exclusively and is based on an applicant's performance on NALA-administered tests.

To sit for the NALA tests, prospective CLA candidates must first meet one of the requirements listed below.

- Graduation from an ABA-approved legal assistant course or graduation from a legal assistant training course at a school that is institutionally accredited

- Graduation from a legal assistant course neither approved by the ABA nor institutionally accredited, plus two years of on-the-job experience
- A bachelor's degree in any field plus one year of experience as a legal assistant
- Seven years of law-related experience under the supervision of a member of a bar (this option is viable only through December 31, 1991)

The designation is granted after successful completion of a comprehensive two-day exam that covers communications, ethics, human relations and interviewing techniques, judgment and analytical ability, legal research, legal terminology, and substantive law. The substantive law section is divided into the following nine subsections: general practice, bankruptcy law, corporate law, estate planning and probate, contract law, litigation, real estate law, criminal law, and administrative law. The examinee takes the general practice section and selects four of the remaining eight specialty tests. To maintain the CLA designation, evidence of continuing legal education must be submitted every five years.

Paralegals who have earned the CLA designation are eligible for NALA's specialty certification. To be certified as a specialist, a paralegal must pass a 4-hour exam in his or her specialty area. Specialty certification is given in the areas of civil litigation, probate and estate planning, corporate and business law, criminal law and procedure, and real estate.

Worth noting: employers often advertise for certified paralegals when they really want paralegals with certificates—not CLA designations.

Because paralegal education and training programs have not been adopted industry-wide, entry into the field is available through a variety of programs to individuals with a wide range of experiences. But it's clear that a combination of formal paralegal education, on-the-job training, and good communication skills—as well as a dose of common sense—will provide you with all the tools you need to succeed in this challenging and rewarding field. And, although this chapter has only touched on the importance of computer literacy, it is an area of expertise that will become more vital to the profession in the years to come. For that reason, the next chapter is devoted entirely to that element of paralegal education.

Taking the Byte out of Computers
Computer Basics for Paralegals

The art of progress is to preserve order amid change and to preserve change amid order.

Alfred North Whitehead

Imagine that you're a paralegal with several years of experience behind you. You've just begun a new job working for a major corporation. One of your primary responsibilities is to administer the company's executive stock option program, which has recently been converted from a manual system to a microcomputer. Although your specialty is in the area of stock options, you don't know anything about computers. (Also, the attorneys know less than you do about them and have no desire to learn—that's why they hired you.) To make matters worse, you learn you won't be receiving any computer training from the company and are expected to figure out what you have to do on your own. You sit down at the computer and turn it on. Unfortunately, the software vendor whose program you are using provides minimal customer support, and the user manual is sketchy, outdated, couched in computerese, and not much help. The test of wits between you and the machine begins. You try every combination of keystrokes but are met with obnoxious bells, buzzers, and flashing lights—all signifying ERROR!

This is the wonderful world of computers you've heard so much about?

Meanwhile, the controller of the company is waiting for a printout of officers' stock options, which the computer supposedly generates in less than 5 minutes. Three hours later the controller has his report, you have ten more gray hairs, and the thought of heading to the nearest exit enters your mind.

You persevere, however. After several more hair-raising episodes over the next few months, not only do you learn how to use the computer, but it becomes your friend and ally. Ultimately, you become a full-fledged computer junkie—you're hooked!

The use of computers in the practice of law has created one of the fastest-growing areas of paralegal specialization. Individuals with computer skills who enter the paralegal field today are one step ahead of the game. Most paralegals will work with computers at some point in their career.

The Legal Profession Discovers Computers

Lawyers are interested primarily in practicing law, and decisions in other business areas, including management, personnel, and operational systems, are often put on a back burner. As such, the legal profession has been comparatively slow to implement the use of computers in its day-to-day operations. The first pioneers brought them into the law office around 1970, and, since then, integration has occurred in three phases.

The first phase occurred between 1970 and 1980 and was marked by the purchase of word processing and billing system equipment on an "as needed" basis, without planning for totally compatible systems, as is generally done today.

The current standard system for word processing in a law firm developed in this period. With it, documents over ten pages are sent to the word processing center, where keyers input them, while documents under ten pages are handled by a secretary. The arrangement provides attorneys with a quick turnaround time and frees up secretaries for other tasks. This allows law firms to charge clients an hourly rate for word processing and can be extremely profitable.

Just as significant as the introduction of word processing was the introduction of computerized billing systems. As discussed in earlier chapters, accurate recording of billable hours for attorneys, paralegals, and support staff is crucial to a firm's profitability. As caseloads increased and clients demanded more detailed invoices, the need for efficient billing systems became apparent. Since these systems ran on expensive mainframes and minicomputers, they were initially purchased by the larger law firms.

(Today, they can run on PCs—personal computers—and are used by firms of all sizes.)

As the decade moved toward the 1980s, firms began to purchase more sophisticated equipment: optical character readers, computerized telephone systems, facsimile machines, laser printers, computerized legal research systems such as LEXIS and WESTLAW, and photocopiers that track client charges. Computerized litigation support systems also emerged in this period. These systems make it possible to do a rapid electronic search through thousands of documents to locate information that can be used in preparation for a trial. They are particularly cost-effective for large cases where a manual search for the same information can take days or weeks.

The second phase of integration occurred between 1981 and 1985 and was characterized by the arrival of the PC. The relatively low cost of this technology made it possible to computerize the office systems of small firms and the sole practitioners that couldn't afford expensive mainframes.

In this second phase, the first systems transferred to PCs were word processing, billing, accounting, research, litigation support, calendaring, and case management. This phase also implemented the concept of networking several PCs together using local area networks (LANs). In this configuration, several secretaries can share the same printer, modem, and software.

The third phase of integration began in 1985 and is still going on. It is perhaps the most exciting and creative of all and is characterized by the development of software for substantive practice areas of law, such as estate planning, corporate, probate, and real estate. It is in this phase that, with programs geared to practice-related tasks, lawyers themselves began to interact directly with computers.

For example, an attorney who specializes in estate planning might use WILLMAKER, a software program developed by Nolo Press/Legisoft to prepare wills. WILLMAKER uses an easy-to-use, menu-driven fill-in-the-blank format to take the user step-by-step through the process of creating a will.

Before I explain some of the applications of computers to the practice of law and how they relate to the responsibilities of paralegals, I want to give you some computer basics.

Computers 101

There are three sizes of computers: mainframes (the most powerful), minicomputers, and PCs (also known as microcomputers).

Advances in technology have led to the development of PCs as powerful as minicomputers. What once took up a whole room can now sit on a desktop and is available at a fraction of the original cost.

The PC is the computer paralegals use most often. It is composed of two parts—hardware and software. The hardware is the physical part of the machine's configuration and includes the monitor, keyboard, central processing unit, hard or disk drives, printer, and modem. The modem is one of the newest and most exciting additions to PC hardware in recent years. It allows data to be transmitted from computer to computer over telephone lines. Once a modem is installed, the user has the ability to instantly access information from thousands of databases (for a fee, of course!) across the country.

Software is the program that tells the computer what to do when. It can be either system software or applications software. System software, such as MS-DOS or PC-DOS, performs basic functions—reading commands from the keyboard to the display screen, preparing disks, and managing disk space—and enables the computer to run applications software. Applications software is a general business program that can be applied to any area of business and falls into one of three categories: word processing, spreadsheet, and database. More specific applications software is available as well and can perform an endless variety of tasks and functions for areas ranging from the practice of law or medicine to video games.

What Paralegals Should Know

Accessing legal databases, maintaining litigation support systems, using general business programs, and developing specific practice area systems all require varying levels of computer skills. Because more and more employers are looking for paralegals with some computer experience, possessing basic skills—including understanding simple jargon and knowing how to execute basic operating systems commands and standard word processing, spreadsheet, and database application programs—is a plus in the current job market.

In addition, paralegals should familiarize themselves with more advanced operating system commands and the various computer products and systems on the market. In this way, once on the job, they can help in the design, selection, and implementation of total computer systems.

The most advanced level of computer literacy is proficiency in the use of programming languages, such as BASIC, COBOL, and Pascal. While most paralegals don't use this kind of expertise on a daily basis, it can be used to design customized programs for substantive practice areas.

As I said earlier, attending a paralegal training program that requires computer literacy courses is the best way to start. If you're working already, however, and want to become computer literate in a hurry, there are several ways to accomplish it: college courses, all-day seminars, on-site training, software tutorials,

---

Ten Helpful Hints

The following axioms may be helpful to remember when you're dealing with computers.

- Computers are a fact of life. No matter how much you resist, eventually you'll be required to learn how to use them. Don't fight it!
- It's difficult to keep up with the myriad products introduced by the computer industry each week—don't even try.
- Every piece of hardware and software is different, and most require trial-and-error training. (Surprisingly, this is the method used by the most experienced computer professionals.)
- Computer training is not a given. Request it from your company or law firm—if you don't ask for it, you may not get it.
- Don't be surprised if you don't understand everything about computers after you receive training. You will.
- Attorneys generally know less about computers than you do and will rely on you to become the expert.
- You don't need to type fast to develop good computer skills.
- The user manual doesn't explain everything. Inevitably, the thing you most need to know won't be in it.
- When you think nothing else could possibly go wrong, be assured that it always will. When first learning how to use a computer, factor in extra time to get the job done.
- Don't get discouraged. Persistence pays off!

---

and, as a last resort, the software manual. I prefer an intensive, all-day seminar supplemented with practice exercises to do on your own over a period of several weeks. College courses are less expensive, but they tend to drag on over the course of a semester. On-site training is great, but companies and law firms generally are reluctant to foot the bill. Software tutorials from user manuals are okay for beginners, but they are limiting—you can't ask a computer questions.

Whatever approach works for you, remember, practice and consistency are the keys.

Computers and the Paralegal

Paralegals are among a law firm's most intensive computer users. The on-the-job applications commonly encountered by paralegals today include:

- Legal and factual research
- Litigation support systems
- Use of general business programs
- Use of legal specialty area programs

Of course, the specific applications used depend on where the paralegal works—a law firm, corporation, or government agency to name a few—his or her legal specialty, the degree of automation within the organization, and, more important, the organization's attitude toward automation. Most of the applications covered in this section are performed on PCs. (While some paralegals may use word processing programs, they are not included in this discussion. I've assumed that paralegals have access to a secretary or a word processing center for those tasks.)

Research

There are two types of computer-assisted research conducted by paralegals—legal and general information (or factual). The information that is sought would be in an on-line database and accessed via modem for a fee.

Legal research. As you learned in Chapter 3, legal research is a search for authorities in the law—more specifically, a search for statutes or court decisions, or both, from a particular jurisdiction—that are applicable to a particular legal situation. The substance of a legal search, whether it is conducted traditionally or is computer aided, is always the same. What varies is the method by which it is undertaken.

After a problem is analyzed in terms of predetermined categories, such as torts, negligence, or conspiracy, the traditional method requires going to a law library to locate the books, indexes, and digests that refer to the desired cases. A computer-assisted search begins with an analysis as well, but the follow-up requires using a database.

The major advantage of computer-assisted research is timeliness. If covered by a database, a court decision (or any other information), would be available on-line almost as soon as it is known. While the information would eventually be available in a law library, the time required for printing, publishing, and distribution delays its accessibility.

The two dominant computer-assisted legal databases available today are LEXIS and WESTLAW. Since LEXIS is the system that's used by the majority of paralegals, this discussion will focus on it.

LEXIS was first marketed in 1973 by the Mead Data Corporation. It provided a thorough, fast, and efficient alternative to conventional legal research methods but was met with some resistance by lawyers who couldn't adapt to the idea of conducting legal research electronically.

LEXIS may be accessed either with a dedicated LEXIS terminal or with a PC and modem. It's composed of federal and state databases that are made up of cases and statutes. The researcher inputs a search request of words, phrases, or numbers, and LEXIS searches the applicable databases to retrieve the case or statute "on point" (the case or statute that most closely resembles the one that's being worked on in terms of legal principles). Cases can be retrieved in various formats—full text, partial text, or citation. LEXIS can also be used for cite checking and Shepardizing, as discussed in Chapter 3.

The key to undertaking a thorough search with LEXIS is the ability to come up with a proper search request *before* accessing the database (the longer you're on-line, the more it costs). The search request can be modified to accommodate new ideas, however, once you're on-line. For example, you are asked to find out what the tort liability of corporate officers is. There are three levels on which you could begin your search.

1. *Level 1 search*—By entering the word "tort," 500 cases that contain the word "tort" are retrieved. Obviously, the search is far too general and must be modified.
2. *Level 2 search*—By entering the phrase "tort and officer," 50 cases that contain both these words are retrieved. This is still too many cases to review.

3. *Level 3 search*—By entering the phrase "tort and officer w/10 corporation," 15 cases are retrieved. (The phrase means that the words "tort and officer" appear within ten words of "corporation.") Since this is a manageable number of cases, you can stop the search here.

As you become familiar with LEXIS, it will become easier to formulate the most efficient and cost-effective search strings.

How much and how often a paralegal uses LEXIS depends on two factors: work environment and area of legal specialty. Paralegals who work at law firms generally do more legal research than those employed by corporations or government agencies. This is because in law firms paralegals work for several clients simultaneously and are more apt to use LEXIS on a daily basis. Those employed by corporations or government agencies usually work with outside counsel, and that counsel does the majority of the research.

The paralegal's specialty area also plays a significant role in determining how he or she uses LEXIS. Many paralegals first encounter LEXIS while working in litigation, since it depends heavily on case law and precedent. In this area, LEXIS is used to search for statutes and case law, to cite check, and to Shepardize.

LEXIS can also be used by paralegals who specialize in securities, probate, tax law, patents, or trademarks. For instance, the LEXPAT database, which contains information on hundreds of patents and trademarks, can be used to do a patent search.

Computer-assisted research is being used by attorneys and paralegals more than ever today, due in large part to expanded databases, reduced on-line costs, and increased acceptance of the technology by the legal profession in general. It has by no means replaced the traditional method—there are many books and periodicals that have not yet been converted to electronic databases—but is seen as an adjunct and supplement to it. Many more years will pass before the law library becomes obsolete. Until that time, paralegals will be required to use both methods of legal research.

General information research. In addition to legal research, the paralegal also conducts factual research. There are over 4,000 on-line databases currently available, though the two most common are NEXIS, which contains magazine and newspaper articles, and the New York Times Information Bank. All of them are available via subscription and provide access to a wide variety of sources for business, education, technological, science, health, and travel information, as well as to the full text of articles from many newspapers and magazines.

The information in these databases can be extremely useful to the practice of law. For instance, if an attorney wanted to know if the firm's client, General Motors, had been mentioned in the news during the last six months in reference to a potential takeover by Ford, a paralegal could scan the *New York Times* and *Wall Street Journal* databases for articles referring to General Motors and Ford.

Litigation Support Systems

Another common computer application used primarily by litigation paralegals is the Automated Litigation Support System (ALSS). It is the computerized method of rapidly managing, accessing, and retrieving information and documents over the course of a lawsuit, and it has changed the practice of litigation. The ALSS has replaced hit-and-miss discovery and trial preparation procedures with more accurate, automated ones.

The ALSS was first developed in the 1970s and ran on large mainframe computers. Today, ALSS's can be run on powerful PCs that operate user-friendly database software programs. Several years ago, the ALSS was recommended only for large cases with 5,000 documents or more, due to high start-up costs. As the price of the more powerful PCs declined, the application of an ALSS to smaller cases became economically feasible. As such, they're now used more frequently.

The primary function of an ALSS is to support the discovery phase of a lawsuit, which, in some cases, can last for years. (Discovery is the tool that allows both parties to discover everything there is to know about the opposition's case.) This is accomplished by using various legal methods, including interrogatories, depositions, document productions, and requests for admissions. The power of an ALSS is its ability to convert the information in these documents to a database for quick access and retrieval.

Two types of ALSS are currently available: document abstract and full text. Document abstract software is used for letters, memos, and any document from which information can be summarized and abstracted. This is done by coding the information by subject matter and entering it into a database.

Full-text software is used when it's necessary to have access to the entire text of a document—a deposition transcript, for example. As mentioned in Chapter 3, summarizing depositions can be tedious and time-consuming. With full-text software, a transcript is transferred to a diskette by a court reporter and then loaded into a computer. The summary is done quickly and easily by electronically scanning the full text for key words and phrases. Many ALSS's combine both document abstract and full-text features.

A paralegal's responsibilities in the development, implementation, and maintenance of an ALSS vary depending on the resources of the law firm and its size, the complexity of the case, the attorneys' attitudes toward paralegals, and the number of support staff assigned to the ALSS project. Duties can range from simple information classification and coding to subjective, substantive analysis of documents.

An ALSS may be purchased off the shelf or custom-built from any one of the general database management systems that are available today. The following example illustrates the role of a paralegal in the development and implementation of a custom-made system.

Creating an ALSS

Once the feasibility of an ALSS is decided upon, the first thing to be done is to create a document abstract database. Most of these databases use a coding system that consists of a key word or an alphanumeric code. (If an ALSS has to be purchased, a paralegal may be asked to assist in the selection of the hardware and software.) Next, an attorney compiles a code book of lists of key people, companies, document types, and words that correspond to issues and facts in the case. A coding form is developed from those lists by a paralegal. It corresponds exactly to the fields in the database. The fields include document or Bates number, document location (storage box number), date, document type (letter, memo, graph), author, recipient, document summary, and individuals and companies mentioned in the document.

The next step is document analysis, coding, and input. The coder may be either a paralegal or someone from another level of support staff. The coding may be objective and/or subjective. Objective coding is limited to the information that appears on the document, such as date, author, and recipient, while subjective coding involves a substantive analysis of its content. The coder reads each document, extracts the relevant information, lists it on the coding form, and inputs the information into the appropriate database fields. At this stage, a paralegal may be responsible for reviewing the work of the coders to maintain quality control.

Once a sufficient database is built, an attorney or paralegal can use the ALSS to retrieve information and hard copy. A paralegal would create and maintain the document retrieval system—an ALSS is of little use if hard copies of the documents referenced in the database can't be located. The retrieval system involves making a working copy of all discovery documents received, Bates stamping them, and filing them chronologically in storage boxes. Once a document has been coded, the hard copy that's been requested can be retrieved from the appropriate storage box by accessing the document location field, which will give the box number. At this point, the paralegal would be using the database software, which requires a more sophisticated level of computer skill.

An ALSS can also be used to support the trial phase of a lawsuit. With the search and sort functions of the database, a paralegal can prepare the witness book and the deposition exhibits that relate to particular witnesses and compile periodic updates to show the status of admitting documents into evidence, and the like.

General Business Programs

Some paralegals have become adept at tailoring general business programs, such as spreadsheet and database management programs, to different areas of legal practice. The application of these programs to tax law, probate law, real estate law, corporate law, and so on, is limited only by the imagination and creativity of the paralegal. Spreadsheet programs are a powerful tool for complex financial, economic, and statistical analysis. Database management programs can be used in litigation for case management and tracking. They can also be used to create billing systems, among other things.

For instance, when I worked as legal administrator for a major corporation I was responsible for the shareholder relations program. This required monthly analysis of the company's shareholder base. Rather than have a transfer agent compile the information for a handsome fee, I prepared the report on an IBM PC using Lotus 1-2-3.

Legal Specialty Area Programs

A recent development in the marriage of computers and law is the trend toward automating tasks and procedures in specific practice areas. This is accomplished with off-the-shelf software or with a system developed in-house. Off-the-shelf software may be used for incorporation, estate administration, drafting wills, fiduciary accounting, or tax applications. The programs take an individual step-by-step through whatever legal process by asking questions and translating the answers into documents. Paralegals who have a combination of computer programming ability and legal skills can sometimes translate their specialty practice areas into custom-designed computer programs. This is a sophisticated use of paralegals and computers, and one that will become more prevalent as paralegals increase their levels of computer expertise and legal knowledge.

Paralegals, Computers, and the Future

In the future, paralegals will be the perfect link between the attorney who knows nothing about computers and the computer specialist who knows nothing about the law. I believe that computer-literate paralegals will become more involved in providing in-house software support, developing new in-house computer applications, and training professional and support staff.

The managers of most law firms now realize that computers can provide them with the competitive edge they need to survive by improving the delivery of legal services, increasing profits, and decreasing personnel and administrative costs. Lawyers who don't integrate computers with their daily practice are at a disadvantage.

There are lawyers who still have mixed feelings regarding computers, however. The difference in attitudes became apparent to me recently when I visited two law firms, each with distinctly different views on the use of computers. The first had PCs in nearly every attorney's office, and the second had *just* installed a dedicated, stand-alone word processing system for the secretaries (remember, these systems have been used by law firms since the early 1970s). When I asked an attorney in the second firm if he used a PC, he replied, "What for?" Old ways and attitudes often die hard. Nevertheless, thanks to the introduction of PCs, individuals who enter the paralegal field today can work in a specialty that didn't exist a decade ago. Computer-literate paralegals will enjoy greater job opportunities, and, as such, increase their prospects for greater job satisfaction.

By now, you have enough information about education, training, skills, and computer expertise to consider a job search. The next chapter demonstrates a number of ways to begin.

Chapter 8

How Do You Find the Right Job?

There is no security on this earth. Only opportunity.

Douglas McArthur

You've now come to one of life's little pleasures: the job hunt. Gone are the days when you could learn a trade, work at one company for thirty-five years, receive a healthy pension, and retire worry free. Many people will change careers—let alone jobs—several times before they retire. Since there are dozens of excellent how-to-land-a-job books on the market that offer valuable advice, I've tried not to be redundant. By offering information related to the paralegal occupation, this chapter begins where those other books leave off.

The Plan of Attack

Developing a plan of attack is an important first step, since the first job that drops into your lap may not be right for you. You should start by identifying the areas of paralegal practice that are most interesting to you. Ultimately, the goal of this plan is to narrow down the choice of possible practice fields to the one that is most in tune with your interests, skills, education, and background. The following four steps will help you achieve that.

Step 1: Summarize the advantages and disadvantages of each field of paralegal practice as you perceive them.

Step 2: Clarify your career goals and objectives by answering important career-related questions.

Step 3: Take a personal inventory of your skills, interests, education, and experiences.

Step 4: Match your goals and objectives with your skills, interests, education, and experiences to determine the best direction for your paralegal job search.

(Before you look at each step in more detail, you may want to review Chapters 2 through 5. They contain information that will help you complete Step 1.)

Step 1: Summarize the Advantages and Disadvantages of Each Practice Field

For illustrative purposes, some of the information from Chapters 3 and 4 has been distilled below to get you started on your summaries. Of course, these examples aren't meant to be exhaustive, and they should be supplemented with information you collect on your own—including any tidbits picked up from conversations you have with working paralegals. Remember that this part of the plan of attack is purely subjective: what is an advantage to me may be a disadvantage to you. These summaries reflect my views. Create your own!

Litigation

Characteristics: Adversarial, court-related tasks, varied cases and clients

Advantages: A good area in which to begin a career, large job market

Disadvantages: Overtime, lots of documentation required, high burnout rate

Potential Employers: Law firms, corporations, banks, insurance companies, government agencies

Comments: In litigation, a paralegal's responsibilities vary depending on the size of the case. Small cases provide a wide variety of duties. On large, more complex, cases, paralegals spend a majority of their time summarizing depositions and preparing document productions.

Computerized Litigation

Characteristics: Court-related tasks, computer oriented

Advantages: Fast-growing specialty area, many employment opportunities projected, high salary potential, career mobility

Disadvantage: Entry-level positions involve tedious coding tasks

Potential Employers: Medium-sized to large law firms

Comments: The size of the law firm you want to work in is an important factor when considering employment in this specialty area. Some law firms don't have the resources to own and operate computerized litigation systems. Experienced paralegals in this field perform functions that require a high level of computer expertise, such as designing and implementing ALSS's.

Family Law

Characteristics: People oriented, involves psychology and sociology, court-related tasks

Advantage: Involves resolution of marital and family-related problems

Disadvantages: Emotional elements, low salary potential

Potential Employers: Small law firms, state and local agencies

Comments: Because medium-sized and large firms do not generally specialize in family law, most jobs in this field are in small firms. Small firms usually have fewer resources than larger ones.

Criminal Law

Characteristics: Involves psychology, sociology, and criminal justice; court-related tasks

Advantage: Diverse cases and clients

Disadvantages: Emotional elements, adversarial, low salary potential, high burnout rate

Potential Employers: Small law firms, district attorney and public defender offices

Comments: While the work is interesting, salaries tend to be lower than in other practice fields, and the burnout rate is higher. Some experts don't believe this to be a good area for a long-term paralegal career.

Corporate Law

Characteristics: Involves business, no court-related tasks

Advantages: Not adversarial, high salary potential

Disadvantage: Less varied work

Potential Employers: Corporations and law firms of all sizes

Comments: The pace of corporate law tends to be less frenetic and stressful than in many other practice areas. However, some paralegals find the work less interesting. Corporate law is a good area for paralegals who are interested in moving into other business careers.

Securities Law

Characteristics: Subspecialty of corporate law, involves financ and investments, no court-related tasks, requires a high leve' responsibility

Advantages: Specialization area, high salary potential

Disadvantage: Small job market

Potential Employers: Medium-sized to large law firms and corporations

Comments: Many experts consider securities law to be an excellent area for individuals interested in a long-term paralegal career. It can also provide a good foundation for the pursuit of other careers in business.

Real Estate Law

Characteristics: Few court-related tasks, requires a high level of responsibility

Advantages: Specialization area, high salary potential

Disadvantage: Small job market

Potential Employers: Law firms, corporations, and real estate development companies

Comments: Real estate law is often likened to securities law in that it is a good area for a long-term paralegal career. It can also provide a good foundation for the pursuit of nonparalegal careers in real estate sales or management.

Estate Planning/Probate

Characteristics: Involves accounting and investment and, therefore, working with numbers; court-related tasks; requires a high level of responsibility

Advantages: Specialization area, excellent for free-lance paralegals, high salary potential

Disadvantage: Small job market

Potential Employers: Law firms of all sizes

Comments: More paralegals have successfully started their own businesses specializing in this area than in any other. Some paralegals believe that this area allows the greatest utilization of their talents and skills.

Bankruptcy

Characteristics: Court-related tasks

Advantages: Specialization area, high salary potential

Disadvantages: Small job market, emotional elements

Potential Employers: Law firms of all sizes

Comments: Employment opportunities in the bankruptcy field tend to be cyclical and depend on the economic conditions that prevail in the nation, region, state, and locality at the time.

Intellectual Property

Characteristics: Few court-related tasks; involves patents, copyrights, and trademarks; requires technical expertise

Advantages: Specialization area, high salary potential

Disadvantage: Small job market

Potential Employers: Law firms and corporations

Comments: Few paralegals are hired to work exclusively in this area. Those who are usually work for large corporations or law firms that specialize in the field.

Labor Law

Characteristics: People oriented, court-related tasks, contact with administrative agencies

Advantage: Specialization area

Disadvantage: Emotional elements

Potential Employers: Law firms and corporations

Comments: Paralegals with expertise in this area can move on to become arbitrators and mediators—jobs that don't necessarily require a law degree but do require a certain kind of legal expertise.

Employee Benefits—Employee Retirement Income Security Act (ERISA)

Characteristics: Requires a high level of responsibility, no court-related tasks

Advantages: Fast-growing specialization area, high salary potential

Disadvantage: Small job market

Potential Employers: Law firms and corporations

Comments: Many experts believe this is a great area to specialize in—if you can find a job. Due to the "graying" of America and changing retirement laws, this specialty will continue to grow.

Workers' Compensation

Characteristics: People oriented, contact with administrative agencies

Advantage: Specialization area

Disadvantage: Small job market

Potential Employers: Law firms and corporations

Comments: The scope of paralegal responsibilities in this area has increased recently, especially in California, which now allows paralegals to represent clients at workers' compensation board hearings.

As you pull together your own summaries, it may be worth noting that the major difference I found between litigation and all other specialty areas is that litigation centers on disputes. You're always trying to prove that you're right and/or that the other person is wrong. This gives the work an adversarial feel that simply does not exist in other practice areas. Some paralegals and attorneys thrive on this and find it stimulating; others find it stressful and draining. Be realistic about the kinds of challenges you want. In addition, if you're considering a long-term career, it's important to know that one of the keys to greater compensation and job satisfaction is the ability to specialize. Look at the preceding pages again. The areas of computerized litigation, securities, probate, ERISA, and real estate provide excellent opportunities for specialization.

 Career Profile

From Nurse to Paralegal

"I received my bachelor's degree in nursing in 1977 and worked for six years as an operating room nurse at Harris Hospital in Fort Worth, Texas. In the summer of 1982, I read an advertisement for a nurse/legal assistant at the law firm of Darrell Keith in Fort Worth. Further inquiry led me down the road I have followed for the last several years—medical malpractice litigation. My plans are to continue in this field. I find great fulfillment combining my background as a nurse with the responsibilities of a legal assistant. Based on my experience, I recommend that any nurse who is considering a nurse/legal assistant career take one or more paralegal courses at a local college. This would provide a fundamental understanding of common legal terminology, which would assist in making the transition."—E. Earl Hauss, senior nurse/legal assistant, Dallas, Texas.

Step 2: Clarify Your Goals and Objectives

In most career guides, "clarify your goals and objectives" is a buzzword phrase that translates to "know thyself." The task is easier said than done. In this chapter, goals and objectives are defined in terms of the specific things that need to be considered when trying to land a job as a paralegal. The following questions will help you identify them.

1. What area of law are you most interested in—corporate, litigation, probate, real estate, patents and trademarks, estate planning, securities, administrative, or criminal law?

2. Do you want to perform court-related tasks or work in a less court-oriented field, such as real estate or intellectual property?

3. Are you interested in an area that is people oriented, such as labor, criminal, or family law?

4. Would you rather start off as a specialist in a large law firm or begin as a generalist in a small firm and decide about your specialization later on?

5. Are you interested in working in the private sector (a law firm, corporation, bank, or insurance company, for example) or in the public sector (a federal, state, or local government agency)?

6. What size law firm do you want to work in—small, medium, or large? (Remember that the larger the firm, the more resources it generally has, which is a plus. However, large firms often want their paralegals to specialize in a particular area, which can be a minus. You could be pigeonholed as someone who can do only a few things well. Small firms have fewer resources and the paralegals that work in them often have a wide range of responsibilities.)

7. What do you want out of a paralegal position? Are you interested in it as a long-term career, as a stepping-stone to a nonparalegal career, or as a stopover on your way to law or business school? (You may not be able to answer this question until you're actually working as a paralegal. Meanwhile, the next chapter discusses the advancement opportunities and options open to all paralegals, and it may help you for now.)

Step 3: Take a Personal Inventory of Your Skills, Interests, Education, and Experiences

After you've determined your goals and objectives regarding a paralegal career, the next step is to assess your education, skills, work experience, and, most important, your interests.

Are you fresh out of high school or college and looking to build a new career? Are you tired of your current job and considering changing careers? Are you returning to the work force after several years' absence and looking to acquire new skills?

As I said earlier, trying to figure out who you are and what you enjoy doing (in terms of work, that is) isn't easy. However, a little preplanning can help you design a more satisfying career. First, you should answer the following questions related to the kinds of skills paralegals use.

1. Do you (or would you) enjoy working independently with minimal supervision?

2. Do you have the capability to handle several projects simultaneously without panicking? Are you able to prioritize?

3. Do you have good verbal and written communication skills?

4. Do you enjoy doing research? Are you able to find information without being told step-by-step how to locate it?

5. Are you detail oriented? Do you have good organizational skills?

6. Are you computer literate? If not, would you be willing to learn computer skills and develop them?

Step 4: Match Your Goals and Objectives with Your Skills, Interests, Education, and Experiences

By matching your goals and objectives to your skills and interests, you should be able to determine the types of paralegal positions that would best suit you.

For instance, let's say you're a recent college graduate with a B.S. in chemistry, and you have worked for the past year in the research and development department of a corporation. You're bored and want to change careers. You're contemplating going to law school and believe some experience as a paralegal would help you make that decision. Your experience, skills, and education make you well suited to a job as a patent paralegal in a corporate law department.

Or perhaps you've been a nurse for the past ten years and want to change careers. You still want to use your medical knowledge and experience, if possible. A position in the area of personal injury law in a small law firm would be an excellent choice.

Suppose you're contemplating returning to the work force after raising a family but feel that you have few marketable skills. You had some secretarial experience years ago, but you don't want to be a secretary again. You could start out as a litigation paralegal or, if you have some computer skills, work in the area of computerized litigation support. As I said earlier, litigation is an excellent place to start: it can provide a basic foundation in legal procedures, and jobs are more plentiful than in other specialty areas.

Maybe you're interested in real estate and have a license but found that the stress of working in sales isn't for you. You could become a paralegal in the real estate department of a law firm, corporation, or development company. That way, you could stay in the field and not have the pressure that comes with sales.

I know someone who majored in finance, worked as a financial analyst for a few years "crunching numbers," and was totally bored. She went back to school to get a paralegal certificate and is now working in securities law specializing in mergers and acquisitions. She uses her finance background daily and is anything but bored.

The point is, don't discount your prior work experience, skills, or interests when looking for a job as a paralegal. You may be able to use them in a specialty area that could be very rewarding.

 Career Profile

From Writer to Government Paralegal

After graduating in 1975 from the University of San Francisco with teaching credentials in secondary education, Kevin Mann tried to find a teaching job in the Bay Area. His efforts proved fruitless, and he began to work as a free-lance writer. As recounted in the magazine At Issue, *one of his free-lance jobs was with the American Indian Center, a San Francisco–based nonprofit agency that provides social services and legal referrals for Native Americans.*

He was eventually hired by the center as legal caseworker and worked primarily on a case involving the relinquishment of parental rights of an Indian family. He left the center after six years. Capitalizing on his experience and interest in the law, in 1982 Mann obtained a paralegal certificate from San Francisco's Heald Paralegal Training Center. Soon after, he began working as a free-lance paralegal for a sole practitioner.

Three years later, Kevin heard about a position in the U.S. Court of Appeals for the Ninth District and was hired as an administrative aide. Today he works for the U.S. Department of Justice's Lands and Natural Resources Division in San Francisco, which handles civil and criminal enforcement cases for the Environmental Protection Agency. Kevin performs paralegal duties and serves as the office manager for his unit, with responsibility for the computer systems. He plans on remaining in the paralegal field and believes that administration represents an excellent career area for paralegals.

Resumes and Cover Letters

As legal administrator for a large San Francisco corporation, I received dozens of resumes and cover letters for clerical, paralegal, and attorney positions within the legal department, and I want to offer a few suggestions about them.

- Keep your resume to one page.
- Check and recheck for misspelled words. Spelling errors are detrimental and very unprofessional—particularly if you're applying for a position that requires excellent writing skills.
- Don't list hobbies on your resume. This is okay for high school students applying for summer work, but not for professionals.
- Don't be verbose. Keep things short and sweet. You can embellish later on in the interview.
- Don't send a standardized cover letter. Express interest in the organization and some knowledge of it. Be personable.

Sources of Employment

After you've determined the best direction for your job search, the next step is to identify the employers who might hire you. Various resources exist to help you.

Classified Ads

Many career guides advise you to stay away from the classified ads, and, for the most part, they are right. However, there are two good reasons why you shouldn't discount them as a source of paralegal employment information.

1. Lawyers advertise to recruit clerical staff, paralegals, and attorneys all the time. Why? Because they're cost conscious and would rather advertise than pay an employment agency.
2. Classified ads can be a valuable source of information, particularly when you begin your job search. You can discover all kinds of facts about employers, legal specialty areas, job

duties, qualifications, salary, and so on. Note the following examples.

Below is a sample ad for a small law firm that is looking for a paralegal to work on large litigation cases using a computerized litigation system. While the position does not require a bachelor's degree, it does require a paralegal certificate.

Seven-attorney law firm seeks paralegal with at least two years of experience and solid complex business litigation background. Exposure to insurance coverage litigation cases and the use of computerized document support systems a plus. A strong sense of responsibility and superior communication and organizational skills a must. Paralegal certificate preferred.

This is an example of an ad that emphasizes experience and communication skills over education. It doesn't state that a bachelor's degree or a certificate is required.

Medium-sized law firm with significant real estate practice seeks a legal assistant with three to four years of experience in the real estate field, with emphasis on major transactions. Knowledge of California corporate and real estate law essential. Considerable client contact. High level of responsibility and independence required. Organization and communication skills critical.

The following ad emphasizes that *everything* is required for this job—experience, skills, a bachelor's degree, and a paralegal certificate.

Participate as an integral member of client team consisting of partner, associate, and paralegals. On this team you will work closely with designated client base through all phases of corporate support, including financing, acquisition, and sale of assets. Corporate formation and maintenance skills necessary. Ideal candidate should have up to four years of experience. B.A. and certificate preferred.

Many paralegals have obtained jobs by answering ads. In fact, I have. After three and a half years as a securities paralegal in a first-rate law firm, I wanted to work in a corporation. As I went about my job search, a counselor at an employment agency told me that finding such a position would be "extremely difficult." That didn't discourage me though. After several months, I was hired by a large corporation—a job I found by answering an ad in a San Francisco legal trade paper. Classified ads *do* work!

The Hidden Job Market

Experts say that only 20 percent of the positions in the general job market are advertised. However, due to the legal profession's propensity to use ads to recruit, I believe the percentage is higher for paralegal and other legal positions. Nevertheless, the hidden job market represents all those employers who don't advertise. It's up to the job hunter to find out who and where they are.

Luckily, this is less difficult than it may sound. If you're interested in working at a law firm, the best place to start your search is with *Martindale-Hubbell*, the bible of the legal profession. The multivolume set of books lists the names, addresses, and telephone numbers of all lawyers and law firms in the country by state and city and is found in every law library. If you want to work at a *particular* corporation, you'll need to get the name and title of its chief legal officer to contact him or her. There are a number of directories in your local library, such as *Standard & Poor's Corporate Records* or Dun & Bradstreet's *Million Dollar Directory,* that provide that information and other valuable facts about the company.

Obtaining a position from the hidden job market requires patience, time, and effort. During my search for a position in a corporation, I sent my resume to the general counsels of the dozen major corporations that I had targeted with the help of the books mentioned above. I followed up with telephone calls but, unfortunately, received no interviews. A year later, while at the job I landed through a classified ad, I received a call from the general counsel of one of those corporations. He had kept my resume on file and when a job came up he thought I was suited for, he called. While I wasn't actively looking for a job at that time, he made an offer I couldn't refuse. It included a 30 percent increase in salary and the opportunity to work in new areas.

If you're pressed for time, the hidden job market may not be the best place to search for your first paralegal position. Once you have some experience and can afford the time it takes to work through the process, however, tapping into this resource will open new doors.

Career Profile

From Housewife to Law Student to Paralegal

"At 38 years old, after raising two children, I went back to school to obtain my bachelor's degree in history. Since I had made the dean's list, I applied to and was accepted at law school. Between my first and second years, I found myself free for the summer and enrolled in the University of San Diego's eleven-week paralegal program. I thought it would help me in law school. I loved it and thought, 'Why should I spend two more years going to law school?' So in 1985, I stopped going to law school and began working as a litigation paralegal in a wonderful law firm. I've been at the same firm ever since.

"After working behind the scenes as a paralegal and seeing how unhappy some lawyers are, I'm no longer interested in going back to law school. I've found that age makes no difference. Younger lawyers seem more disillusioned because they thought it would be different. Attorneys tell me, 'You really have the best. You're not sitting on the side of your bed at two in the morning worrying if you did something wrong the day before.' Besides, now that I'm 48, I have no desire to take time away from my husband and myself by returning to law school."—Diane Remick, senior paralegal, San Diego, California

Employment Agencies

Most of the nationally known employment agencies have legal divisions that recruit legal personnel. However, lacking paralegal experience themselves, many of these recruiters know little, if anything, about the field.

Within the last five years a new breed of employment agency has emerged. For the most part, such agencies are owned and operated by former paralegals and are dedicated solely to placing paralegals. The main advantage of these agencies is that their recruiters, as former paralegals, know and understand the needs and concerns of the employer *and* the employee. I strongly recommend using this type of agency over the traditional kind, whose recruiters may not know a paralegal from a parakeet.

When a friend of mine was laid off after working for eight years at a large San Francisco corporation, she went to a regular agency

123

to help her find temporary positions. Her specialty was regulatory law and her resume showed quite clearly that she was highly skilled and experienced. She had also worked as a litigation paralegal for six years, which gave her a total of fourteen years of experience. When she interviewed for a temporary assignment, the recruiter wasn't sure if summarizing depositions (a *basic* skill) would be too difficult for her level of experience!

An agency owned and run by paralegals is better equipped to match a person's skills and experience with the level required by a particular position. To locate such agencies, contact your local paralegal association. It's likely to have a list of them.

Temporary assignments. While paralegal employment agencies offer permanent and temporary placement services, temporary assignments are an excellent way to obtain your first paralegal job. They give you the opportunity to gain valuable experience and test the waters before jumping in headfirst. Temping enables you to work at several different law firms or corporations before deciding what's best for you. And organizations often offer permanent positions to temporary workers, which is what happened to Chyllene Cattie, a paralegal at Dechert, Price and Rhoads in Philadelphia.

"Although I received my paralegal certificate in September 1985, I actually started working a few months before I received it. A temporary paralegal agency in Philadelphia had a position that needed someone with computer knowledge," she says. "Since I had prior experience training people on computers, they placed me in it. It involved computerized litigation for a large antitrust case. After three months, the firm realized there wasn't enough work to employ me full-time on that one case, so they began giving me other cases. Nine months later, they bought me out of my contract, and I have been here ever since."

Temporary assignments benefit employers as well as employees. Since the recession of the early 1980s, many companies have cut staffing to the bare bones to reduce expenses. They have remained reluctant to increase the size of their permanent staff. Law firms are no different. In fact, the work that comes into law firms tends to be cyclical, which makes temporary employees an essential part of the work force. They are hired on an as-needed basis.

Promotions

Because more than 31 percent of the paralegals who responded to the NFPA's 1988 survey had some experience as legal secretaries before becoming paralegals, this alternative route to the profession can't be overlooked. However, it's more than likely that most of those individuals began working in law firms many years ago, as did Royanne Hollins, senior paralegal at Matheny, Poidmore & Sears in Sacramento.

"I have been working in a medium-sized law firm in Sacramento for the past twelve years and began my legal career here as a green, inexperienced legal secretary," she says. "I performed many paralegal duties while maintaining my responsibilities as legal secretary. Holding down two jobs and getting paid for only one was an incentive to complete a paralegal certificate program." Currently the senior civil litigation paralegal in charge of paralegal staffing, hiring, and firing, Royanne also runs the computerized litigation support system and performs all of her original paralegal duties. "In 1988, I sat down with my boss and discussed the possibility of attending law school," she states. "I'm now attending law school at night and look forward to taking the California bar in 1992."

Today, there are still a good many paralegals who, like Royanne, began as a legal secretary. However, as stated in Chapter 6, the growing popularity of the profession and the large pool of available certified or degreed paralegals make that kind of "in" less likely.

Placement Services

Most reputable paralegal programs have placement services for new graduates and alumni. Law firms often use them to recruit new paralegals. If you're attending one of these programs or have graduated from one, be sure to check out this option.

 Career Profile

From Accountant to Paralegal

"I received a bachelor's degree in accounting and worked as an accountant for two years. I was bored silly because there was not enough contact with people. Then I moved to Boulder, Colorado, and didn't know what I wanted to do, so I worked for a while as a cook in a restaurant. When a friend of mine suggested that I'd make a good paralegal, I started looking into paralegal schools. I chose the one that would give me the broadest base of knowledge. I loved

it! I went two days a week while I continued to work. Part-time, it took two years to complete.

"After the first year of school, the Manville Corporation was hiring temporary paralegals to work on a large asbestos case. I worked for it while I finished the program. While at Manville, I continued to look for a job and was hired by an insurance company's legal department. I spent two years with it doing corporate work but had the feeling that I really wanted to do litigation. I interviewed with Davis, Graham & Stubbs in Denver and was really impressed with the fact that they were more concerned about whether Davis, Graham was right for me, and not vice versa. I was hired to work in the product liability group.

"From the beginning, I knew exactly what I wanted in a paralegal position—one where I was the attorney's right hand, where I would be involved in everything, and where I would be respected as part of the team. I think that's what everyone wants. I feel fortunate to have attained it."—Ingrid Tronsrue, paralegal, Denver, Colorado

Internships

Internships are usually incorporated into paralegal certificate programs and offer the student an opportunity to gain on-the-job skills and experience. Many times a law firm will hire an intern after he or she has completed the program.

If you haven't graduated from a program that offers internships and you haven't had any luck landing an entry-level job, volunteering your services free for a limited amount of time can give you a leg up. If you can do it, this is the kind of experience that will help you land your first job.

Networks

If you're new to town or are switching careers and don't know anyone local who's in the field, networking can be quite difficult. The easiest way to tap into the paralegal scene is to join the local paralegal association. These associations have a lot of valuable information and resources—including newsletters, career forums and seminars in various practice areas, and job hot lines. Most are also members of the NFPA, which publishes a quarterly newsletter that you'll receive when you join at the local level. Also, keep in mind that the legal community in most cities, even the larger ones, is relatively small and close-knit. Once you start networking, you'll get to know a lot of people in a short amount of time.

What Do Employers Want?

Since the profession has yet to define standards for education and training that have been accepted industry-wide, the requirements for paralegal jobs vary from employer to employer.

Some of the factors lawyers consider when hiring paralegals are contained in a study on paralegal licensing and certification that was conducted by the ABA's Standing Committee on Legal Assistants in 1984. Over 330 attorneys from forty-six states responded to the survey, representing 300 law firms, corporations, and agencies. The criteria included:

- Graduation from an ABA-approved paralegal program
- Graduation from any paralegal program
- A bachelor's degree
- An associate degree
- Law office experience
- Experience in a particular law firm

Attorneys were asked to determine whether a particular criterion was mandatory for hiring paralegals, a major factor, important, a minor factor, or not relevant. Two trends emerged: most attorneys agree that experience in a law office is important when considering candidates, and more emphasis is placed on a bachelor's degree by large firms than small ones. My experiences in the field over the last ten years have shown me that these two trends are accurately stated. I have also found that holding a degree is a plus when trying to win a paralegal job in a corporation. (One of the first questions asked during salary negotiations for both of the corporate positions I held in San Francisco was whether I had a college degree.) Results from the ABA survey are reflected in the table on the following two pages.

Criteria for Hiring Paralegals
(American Bar Association Survey*)

Graduation from an ABA-approved paralegal program. Only 5 percent of all firms felt that graduating from an ABA-approved program was mandatory, while 36 percent felt it was not even relevant. Only 35 percent felt that it was either a major factor or important.

ABA Approval	All Firms %	Large Firms %	Small Firms %
Mandatory	5	14	2
Major factor	12	19	7
Important	23	20	22
Minor factor	24	31	26
Not relevant	36	16	44

Graduation from any paralegal program. Forty-one percent of all firms felt that graduating from any paralegal program was either a major factor or important.

Paralegal Program	All Firms %	Large Firms %	Small Firms %
Mandatory	13	15	13
Major factor	16	13	13
Important	25	30	23
Minor factor	27	35	27
Not relevant	19	7	24

Necessity of a bachelor's degree. Sixty-two percent of large firms felt a bachelor's degree was either a major factor or important compared to 45 percent of all firms and only 38 percent of small firms.

Bachelor's Degree	All Firms %	Large Firms %	Small Firms %
Mandatory	13	23	9
Major factor	18	29	13
Important	27	33	25
Minor factor	24	6	30
Not relevant	18	8	24

Necessity of an associate degree. Forty-one percent of small firms felt that a two-year degree was either a major factor or important compared to only 28 percent of large firms.

Associate Degree	All Firms %	Large Firms %	Small Firms %
Mandatory	6	5	5
Major factor	9	7	8
Important	30	21	33
Minor factor	25	26	28
Not relevant	31	42	28

Law office experience. Sixty-three percent of all firms and 66 percent of large and small firms felt that law office experience was either a major factor or important.

Experience in Any Law Office	All Firms %	Large Firms %	Small Firms %
Mandatory	13	4	20
Major factor	32	37	37
Important	31	29	29
Minor factor	18	19	11
Not relevant	6	10	4

Experience in your own law firm. Forty-nine percent of small firms felt this was either a major factor or important compared to only 38 percent of large firms.

Experience in Your Own Law Firm	All Firms %	Large Firms %	Small Firms %
Mandatory	9	0	15
Major factor	25	19	31
Important	18	19	18
Minor factor	17	27	13
Not relevant	32	35	23

*The figures in this table have been rounded off to the nearest whole numbers. As such, the columns may total more or less than 100 percent.

Some Thoughts About Working with Lawyers

If you've never set foot inside of a law firm or worked for an attorney, there are a few things you should know.

- Lawyers tend to work hard—very hard—and they generally want the same from all other legal personnel. Their expectations of themselves and their staff are extremely high. So be prepared. There's a lot at stake in law. After all, when things go wrong, all eyes turn to the lawyer.

- Lawyers aren't in business to win personality contests. As a result, they may not be the most personable people in the world. They're often preoccupied and in a hurry.

- Lawyers are renowned for giving vague assignments. For instance, when briefing you about the facts in a case, an attorney usually does just that—"brief" you. Typically, they don't have a lot of time (or the patience) to stop and explain things in detail. Consequently, a lot of your learning will come by osmosis and trial and error. (That's why you need to know how to locate information quickly and on your own.)

- Lawyers are notorious for waiting until the last minute to give you an assignment they wanted done yesterday.

- To complete an assignment on time, convert minutes to hours, hours to days, days to weeks, and so on. When a lawyer says, "This will take you only 2 hours to do," be wary! After ten years of hearing statements like that, I can assure you that 2 hours usually means two days.

- There are many good lawyers out there (contrary to the popular notion).

- Lawyers, particularly those from the old school, need to be educated from time to time about what paralegals are capable of doing. You'll have to do it.

Job opportunities are everywhere for paralegals. The field is relatively young; the rate of turnover is high in comparison to other, more established professions; and new positions are being created as more employers discover the benefits of using paralegals.

From personal experiences, I and others in the field can testify that the ways to locate paralegal jobs described in this chapter really do work. Using classified ads, contacting paralegal placement agencies, tapping into the "hidden" job market, and networking are effective ways to find employers who *will* hire you.

Once you obtain your first job and get your foot in the door, it's important to continue to make yourself as marketable as possible. With that in mind, the next chapter looks at the ways in which you can advance your career.

Chapter

9

Where Do You Go from Here?
Career Paths for Paralegals

Success usually comes to those who are too busy to be looking for it.

Henry David Thoreau

Trust officer. Writer. Paralegal manager. Financial analyst. Pension specialist. Personnel director. Journalist. Computer sales representative. Real estate portfolio manager. Land acquisitions supervisor. Legal administrator. Law firm marketing administrator. Securities trainee. Legislative analyst. These are all positions that are held by former paralegals. For paralegals with specialized skills, advancement opportunities are everywhere. How far you go depends on what you do with what you have. As Henry Ford once said, "Whatever you have, you must either use or lose."

In the early days of the profession, before employers recognized the potential of paralegals, the tasks and responsibilities of the job weren't very sophisticated. For many years, one of the most common complaints from working paralegals was the lack of opportunity for advancement. Overworked, underpaid, burned-out paralegals could look only to law school as a way out of what was perceived as a dead-end job. Many left the profession before the applicability of their skills to other fields became apparent.

Things are different today. The ability to specialize has provided paralegals with expanded responsibilities and opportunities for advancement inside and outside of the legal field. For the most part, attorneys have recognized the value of paralegals and are using them for more and more complicated tasks. And employers outside the legal industry have seen the value of their skills,

133

education, and training. As such, the future for paralegals with solid experience is wide open—they have the choice between remaining in the field or using it as a stepping-stone to some other profession. It's a great occupation for someone who wants to be proactive when making career decisions.

As you read this chapter, remember that career growth and satisfaction are subjective qualities. What is challenging and rewarding to you may be boring to someone else. Lynda Wertheim, legal assistant manager at White & Case in New York City, puts it like this: "For some people, all jobs are transitional ones, representing steps in some master personal career plan. For others, any responsibility that can be defined as a job is characterized as dead-end."

Career Tracks

Imagine that you've been working as a paralegal for almost three years. You feel as though you've reached the limits of your present job. You're a little bored and want a new challenge. What can you do? There are a number of alternatives. Since I've done most of them, I've arranged them below in order from the easiest to the most difficult to accomplish.

1. Remain with your current employer and advance to senior paralegal.
2. Remain a paralegal but change your work environment.
3. Remain a paralegal but change your legal specialty area.
4. Assume managerial and supervisory duties.
5. Assume administrative duties.
6. Use your legal skills in a law-related field.
7. Use your legal skills in a non-law-related field.
8. Free-lance and start your own business.
9. Pursue additional education.

Advancing to Senior Paralegal

Assuming that the law firm you're working for offers this career track, advancing to senior paralegal is perhaps the easiest of all the options to pursue. Senior paralegal status is usually found in medium-sized and large law firms and in corporations with very large legal departments. It's an excellent way of rewarding experienced paralegals who are committed to a long-term career. Senior paralegals often assume some managerial and/or administrative responsibilities in addition to their ongoing paralegal duties.

Perquisites for senior paralegals usually include a higher salary scale (from $5,000 to $10,000 more than paralegals), larger bonuses, and more vacation time. Benefits to the employer include the opportunity to bill at a higher rate (which can increase profitability) and also lower paralegal turnover and more satisfied employees (both of which of course mean greater productivity).

Changing Work Environment

After working at a large law firm for over three and a half years, I decided I needed a change. I wanted to use my legal skills in a more generic business environment and take advantage of the benefits a corporation could offer. I landed a job in a corporate legal department. For paralegals who want to remain in the field but need a change of scenery, this track works wonders. Common moves are from large law firms to smaller ones and from law firms to corporations.

As discussed in Chapter 2, working in a corporation has some advantages over working in a law firm. One such may be a higher salary. For paralegals with three or more years of law firm experience who want a slower, less hectic pace, corporations are the answer. Also, if you're thinking about going back to school part-time, most corporations offer some kind of tuition reimbursement plan. Working in a corporation has its disadvantages, too. There may be less job security. With the current frenzy of corporate mergers and acquisitions, you could wake up one morning and find out that the company has been taken over and that you no longer have a job.

Changing Legal Specialty Areas

This alternative takes a bit more effort than changing work environments. My own experience left me believing that such a change is well worth that effort. As I said earlier, after only a year in litigation—even though I was working for great attorneys on cases that were quite interesting—I just wasn't satisfied. Three months after telling the paralegal manager of the firm that I wanted to move out of litigation, I moved into the corporate and securities group. I knew immediately that I had done the right thing. My new responsibilities included the securities filings of small, start-up, high-tech companies. Since the job required that I be in touch with the SEC, underwriters, and investment bankers, it was a great way to learn about the securities industry.

Finding another position with the same law firm is only one way to change legal specialty areas. Other routes include changing firms and taking courses or continuing education seminars in the area of interest.

Assuming Managerial and Supervisory Duties

In 1979, a friend of mine was hired by a small law firm in Hartford, Connecticut, as its first paralegal. As the firm added more attorneys and paralegals, she assumed additional responsibilities, including the coordination and supervision of six paralegals. Today, she coordinates the firm's entire paralegal program and manages more than twenty-five paralegals. By taking on additional duties, she was able to carve out a niche that provided her with a way into management.

Paralegal management is a traditional career move for experienced paralegals. Depending on the size of the firm, some paralegal managers split their time between managerial duties and paralegal duties, while others function solely as managers. Responsibilities include interviewing and recruiting paralegals; coordinating projects and assignments between paralegals; designing, implementing, and maintaining in-house training programs; administering salaries; and evaluating performance. Paralegal managers also function as liaisons between paralegals and other levels of management. This is a delicate role, particularly for managers who continue to perform their regular paralegal duties.

Laurie Roselle, paralegal coordinator at Rogers & Wells in New York City, enjoys the dual role. "I did it on purpose because I firmly believe that you cannot supervise people when you don't know what those people are doing. When I first started working here, they were strictly looking for a paralegal supervisor. I told them I didn't want to lose my paralegal skills, and so we worked out an agreement. When work comes in, I reserve the right to handle it, but I am also responsible for the hiring, firing, and training of over twenty paralegals."

Salaries for paralegal managers are significantly higher than the salaries for senior paralegals. In a 1986 survey conducted by Arthur Young, a "Big 8" accounting firm, the *average* salary for paralegal managers ranged from $33,700 (small law firms) to $45,890 (large firms), while salaries for senior paralegals ranged from $24,294 to $33,179. Paralegal managers working in corporate law departments earned an average of $36,390.

If you're considering this option, remember that not every law firm or corporation has a paralegal management career track.

Assuming Administrative Duties

Administration is considered by some an excellent avenue for career advancement. The two positions commonly associated with this path are legal administrator and law firm marketing administrator.

Legal administrator. Legal administration was formally recognized as a career within the legal industry in 1971, with the inception of the Association of Legal Administrators (ALA). Before that, law office management was delegated to lawyers who often had little interest in administrative matters. Since the competition for clients has heated up, and profitability is a real concern for law firms, the role of the legal administrator has become critical to the business side of law. "Legal administrators are the management generalists in an organization full of specialists," states former ALA President Beverlee Johnson, who's now general manager of Chas. P. Young Management Services in San Francisco. "Our role—planning, integrating, evaluating, motivating—provides the glue that holds the organization's processes and players together."

Over 90 percent of legal administrators work in law firms, 5 percent work in corporate legal departments, and less than 2 percent work in government agencies. A legal administrator manages the planning, marketing, business functions, and operations of a law office. Responsibilities include finance, human resources, computer systems, and facilities planning. A legal administrator might also be involved in other areas of law firm management, including policymaking, business development, attorney recruitment, and legal services marketing. Since legal administration is a managerial career track, the average salary is around $50,000—substantially higher than the average salary for paralegals and paralegal managers.

Legal administrators may be attorneys who are more interested in managing than in practicing law; paralegals or paralegal managers who have taken on additional administrative duties; or professional managers with no legal experience who are recruited because of their expertise in finance, personnel, data processing, marketing, or other business support areas. Because they understand the nature of law firms and the needs of lawyers and clients firsthand, paralegals have an edge in winning these jobs over managers with no legal background. Also, since monitoring a firm's profitability is an important area of legal administration, a paralegal's understanding of billing and tracking time is extremely valuable.

Law firm marketing administrator. This is a new career niche that has emerged in the past few years. Since the rules that govern the use of advertising by lawyers were relaxed by the courts over a decade ago, lawyers have begun to realize the benefits of marketing and advertising their services. With competition for clients keen, the marketing administrator plays a vital role in client development and in a firm's profitability.

Susan Peifer, paralegal coordinator at Gordon & Rees in San Francisco, is a paralegal manager who moved into marketing administration by assuming responsibilities in that area. "I started as paralegal coordinator for a law firm that never had one," she admits. "After one year, the partners began to give me other responsibilities, such as preparing the newsletter and coordinating the firm's anniversary party. It just happened. Once I had a base, I started building on it. In addition to overseeing the in-house paralegal program, I am responsible for the marketing and recruiting functions of the firm.

"On the marketing side, I prepare the firm's monthly newsletter and brochures, as well as coordinate all client development activities and social events. I am also responsible for recruiting on college campuses, which begins in September of each year. You always have to come up with different ways of advertising your services. For instance, I got the idea to have the slogan 'Just Say No to Drugs' and 'Gordon & Rees' imprinted on the trash bags you use in your car. We passed them out everywhere and the response we received was phenomenal," she says.

"For anyone interested in getting into marketing administration, the easiest way is to get your foot in the door as a paralegal or paralegal manager. Once you have a solid position, you can build on it by assuming marketing responsibilities," she concludes.

While some marketing administrators are recruited from the outside—particularly in large firms—in small firms, paralegals often have an advantage over these individuals (as Susan did) when it comes to this position.

Using Legal Skills in a Law-Related Field

Paralegals have an advantage over many other paraprofessionals. Unlike a paramedic, whose skills can be used only in the medical field, a paralegal can use his or her knowledge and skills outside of a law firm or corporate law department in a number of law-related occupations. For instance, a paralegal who has developed expertise in labor law could move into arbitration or mediation, a corporate paralegal could become a corporate secretary, and a litigation paralegal could move into court administration.

Arbitration and mediation. As mentioned in Chapter 1, paralegals who have experience in labor law and labor relations might want to consider a position in arbitration as an alternative career. Arbitration is fast becoming a major way of settling disputes in areas such as labor/management relations, commercial transactions, and, more recently, uninsured motorist and no-fault insurance plans.

In arbitration, each party presents oral testimony, relevant documents, and, sometimes, witnesses at a hearing conducted by an arbitrator. The arbitrator is an impartial person chosen by the parties involved in the dispute and is vested with the power to make the decision (binding on both parties) that will resolve the dispute.

"When parties decide to arbitrate a dispute, by definition they are willing to set the legal entanglements aside in order to obtain a quick and inexpensive resolution," explains Michael West, president of Arbitration West in Los Gatos, California, in an article in *Nolo News.* In California, there is no requirement in the state arbitration law that says an arbitrator must be an attorney. In fact, Mr. West, who is not a lawyer, believes that law school training may be counterproductive to the arbitration process. "We have developed our skills and professional reputations through the ability to be neutral, the ability to conduct a fair and impartial hearing, the ability to discern the truth from the facts presented, and a passion for rendering a fair and equitable decision. Legal training is more or less irrelevant to these qualities. In fact, it can be counterproductive, as arbitration is intended to eliminate legal maneuvering," he states.

You should be aware, however, that the majority of arbitrators are attorneys. As a result, it may be more difficult for paralegals not only to pursue a career in arbitration but to establish credibility in the area. An alternative career to arbitration might be mediation, which is a less formal, nonbinding method of dispute resolution.

Corporate secretary. For paralegals with experience in corporate law, pursuing a position as corporate secretary is a natural choice for career advancement. Corporate secretary is an officer-level position within a corporation that can be filled by a lawyer or a nonlawyer.

After working for four years as a corporate and securities paralegal, I was hired by a large corporation to take on the duties of the corporate secretary. The responsibilities included preparing for board of directors and shareholder meetings, managing shareholder relations program, administering dividend reinvestment and stock option plans, managing proxy solicitation, preparing securities filings, and monitoring insider-trading compliance.

Compensation for corporate secretaries varies greatly depending on the size of the organization, size of staff, geographic location, title of the position, and educational background of the individual. In a 1986 survey conducted by the American Society of Corporate Secretaries, 62 percent of the respondents' salaries were over $45,000.

Court administration. Court administration involves a combination of managerial, administrative, and paralegal duties and is an excellent career move for litigation paralegals who have several years of experience. Since these positions are located in federal, state, and local government agencies, hiring procedures follow stricter guidelines than in the private sector. Responsibilities include the areas of calendar management, case flow procedures, personnel studies, facilities planning, and automation needs assessment. Salaries in major metropolitan areas start anywhere between $35,000 and $40,000, depending on experience.

Government jobs. The federal government employs over 135,000 people in law-related positions. The following is a list of just some of the jobs in government that could be obtained with experience in particular legal specialty areas.

Position	Legal Specialty Area
Mediation specialist	Labor
Labor/management relations examiner	
Criminal investigator	Litigation (criminal)
Clerk of the court	
Realty specialist	Real estate
Land law examiner	
Patent adviser	Intellectual property
Copyright examiner	
Tax law specialist	Tax
Internal revenue officer	
Estate tax examiner	Estate planning/probate

Other law-related jobs in government include equal opportunity specialist, employee relations specialist, labor relations specialist, civil rights analyst, contract administrator, immigration inspector, hearings and appeal officer, legislative analyst, insurance examiner, intelligence analyst, foreign affairs officer, foreign law specialist, international trade specialist, technical information specialist, social insurance administrator, public utilities specialist, and social service representative. Many of these are mid- or senior-level positions. As of 1988, mid-level positions (grades GS-9 through GS-12) ranged in salary from $22,906 to $43,181, and senior positions (grades GS-13 through GS-15) ranged from $39,501 to $71,377. For more information, contact Federal Reports, Inc., in Washington, D.C., at 202-393-3311, which publishes a helpful brochure entitled *The Paralegal's Guide to U.S. Government Jobs: How to Land a Job in 70 Law-Related Areas.*

Investigation. Private investigation is an interesting, but somewhat offbeat, area that uses many of the research skills acquired by paralegals. When Julie Champion, a private investigator in Sacramento, California, finished her paralegal certificate program, she realized that she enjoyed the research component of paralegal work best. Instead of seeking work in a traditional paralegal capacity, she applied for a position as a private investigator. "I always liked to figure out puzzles. I could pick up a mystery novel, read it, and know the answer in a few minutes," she says. "I thought the paralegal field would be interesting because I like to read and do research. But after attending paralegal school, I found I didn't like the paperwork aspect of it. So I took the research and investigative part of paralegal work and applied for positions in the area of private investigation. While most investigators had a law enforcement background, I did not. What I did have was the attitude that I really wanted to learn, plus I knew I had the research skills. I would not take 'no' for an answer, and I was hired as a trainee," she explains.

Julie's job entails 50 percent workers' compensation and personal injury cases and 50 percent homicide cases. Her duties involve meeting with claims adjusters, contacting all the parties involved in a claim, gathering background information and witness statements, preparing reports, taking photographs, and doing surveillance work. She also supervises the investigators and the secretarial staff and is the office administrator.

According to Julie, most of her clients are insurance companies and law firms that specialize in workers' compensation and personal injury cases. "Contrary to popular belief," she offers, "we have very few clients who want their husband or wife investigated." She reports that most investigators work on a contract basis per case and receive anywhere from $10 to $25 per hour and up, depending on the case and type of service. A full-time in-house investigator (usually a former police officer) who works for a law firm can earn $70,000–$80,000 per year. "I definitely see myself staying in the field of investigation," says Julie. "I feel I have a lot more options available to me because of my paralegal degree and investigative background."

Using Legal Skills in a Non-Law-Related Field

Applying your experience and skills as a paralegal to non-law-related professions is an excellent way to advance into a new career.

Computer specialist. The world of technology and computers is wide open to computer-literate paralegals—particularly those who have gone beyond the basics and learned programming languages. The combination of paralegal and computer skills is unbeatable.

Legal industry consulting, particularly in the area of computers and automation, is a growing opportunity for computer-literate paralegals. Many of the large national accounting firms have legal divisions that offer consulting services to law firms. Browsing through the *New York Times* recently, I noticed an ad for one of these firms that read:

Litigation Support Consultant

We are seeking a senior consultant to join the staff of our New York Legal Services Group. This individual will have three years of experience working for a litigation support vendor or for a law firm as a litigation paralegal. Excellent oral and written communication skills and experience with microcomputer software packages are required. A bachelor's degree in English is desirable.

Paralegals can also work as consultants for computer companies such as IBM, Wang, and Digital that market products to the legal industry.

Another career alternative in this area is sales for a company that specializes in legal software applications. Today there are literally hundreds of computer companies that produce software for litigation support, document management, database services, accounting and billing, docket control, and word processing, as well as for specialty practice areas such as tax, probate, and corporate law. Each one of these companies represents a potential opportunity for the computer-literate paralegal.

When I was a legal administrator, I was responsible for finding and purchasing a stock option software package that could be used on the firm's microcomputer. (We had been paying a large monthly fee to a time-share company through which the data were accessed via a modem.) Since I had over four years of experience in stock options and computers, I knew exactly what was needed. When one of the vendors demonstrated a product, I offered some suggestions about how it could be improved. To my surprise, the next day the company's vice president called to offer me a position as West Coast sales representative. I turned the job down, but it goes to show you how far expertise can take you.

An option for paralegals with several years of experience in computerized litigation systems is a position with a litigation support company. Litigation support companies are hired by law firms to provide litigation support, particularly on large cases.

Recruitment. Temporary employment agencies are among the fastest-growing industries today. As discussed in Chapter 8, agencies dedicated solely to the placement of paralegals are a recent phenomenon, and positions within these agencies represent excellent alternatives for paralegals. These agencies differ from traditional employment agencies in that they are usually run by former paralegals who understand not only the paralegal field but also the needs and requirements of law firms.

Denise Templeton is one paralegal who made the transition into the recruitment field. In 1983, she founded the first paralegal employment firm, Templeton & Associates, in Minneapolis, Minnesota. "I thought it would be a good idea to start a temporary paralegal agency that would provide law firms with experienced paralegals rather than those at the entry level," she says. "While we place both permanent and temporary paralegals, most assignments are in the area of litigation, since that's where the biggest need is. We've grown 20 percent per year and just opened an office in Chicago. In addition, we've recently added a legal secretaries division and now offer computerized deposition summary services."

Sales. A career path often overlooked by many paralegals is sales. Besides computer hardware and software products, there are many other services that can be marketed to the legal industry—legal publication sales and photocopy services, for instance.

Companies such as Matthew Bender, Westlaw, and BNA (Bureau of National Affairs) publish books, reports, and updates that are vital to every law library. Companies like these are almost always looking for competent sales representatives who understand the legal industry. Paralegals obviously have an edge over salespeople who don't have legal backgrounds and often don't understand the legal profession. (Keep in mind that most sales positions are based on commissions, which means that what you earn depends on how much you sell.)

Shareholder/investor relations and corporate communications. For paralegals with experience in securities law, shareholder relations is a natural career alternative. As I said earlier, one of my responsibilities as a legal administrator was administration of the company's shareholder relations program. This included monitoring the shareholder base of the company, tracking the number of shares in all stock plans, supervising the stock transfer agent, managing the proxy solicitation process, filing various securities reports, and handling all shareholder communications.

All or part of these duties can also be handled by a corporate communications manager or an investor relations manager. These are two other possible career tracks for paralegals with experience in the corporate and securities areas. A corporate communications department is responsible for all of a company's internal and external communications, including the annual report, press releases, employee newsletters, executive video presentations, and so on. Investor relations involves dealing with the investment community—securities analysts, brokers, and portfolio managers. Many individuals who enter investor relations are seasoned professionals with accounting, finance, or operations backgrounds, or experience in the securities industry. As a result, this is a difficult field for paralegals to enter.

Teaching. Paralegal program administrators are always looking for qualified paralegals to teach a course or two. If you have several years of experience in a particular area and are interested in teaching, you should contact the programs in your area. Although schools often use attorneys to teach paralegal classes, students commonly complain that lawyers focus more on theory than practical skills. Instructors who are paralegals have first-hand experience in the day-to-day realities of the job.

Teaching is an excellent way to increase your professional status and to supplement your income. Most teaching positions are part-time, but with some classroom experience you could work your way into a full-time position as program coordinator or administrator.

Diane Remick, senior paralegal at Stutz, Gallagher & Artiano in San Diego, is an instructor in the University of San Diego's paralegal program. "I started teaching as a result of my position as secretary for the San Diego Association of Legal Assistants. This is my second year teaching. Once you get your class organized and outline prepared, it's enjoyable. I become a different person behind a podium—it's a high. I teach Introduction to Legal Systems two quarters a year on Monday nights. The course is an introduction to everything—civil procedure, legal research, and six other areas of law. Teaching part-time while working full-time gives me the best of both worlds," she explains. "Also, teaching has led to advisory board work for the University of San Diego and the San Diego Community College District as well as a position on the ABA-accreditation team for paralegal education."

Writing. Since paralegals spend most of their time developing writing and research skills, nonfiction writing is a natural career alternative for paralegals, as my own experience demonstrates.

Most nonfiction writers start their careers by getting a few articles published before attempting to write a book. Not so with me. My only published works consisted of one travel article and a letter to the editor of a Bay Area newspaper about the 1988 presidential campaign. Not exactly an impressive list of credentials. But I knew I could write, and I knew I had something to say that hadn't been said before. It was just a matter of convincing a publisher.

However, I don't recommend launching a writing career with a book. Paralegals who are interested in pursuing a writing career might begin by writing an article for either a lawyer or paralegal trade journal on some aspect of the field. Paralegal journals such as *Legal Professional* and the *Journal of Paralegal Education and Practice* are excellent places to begin. Once you get a few articles published, you will have developed a portfolio of writing samples, which could help you land writing jobs in other areas, including journalism, business writing, and technical writing. I do recommend subscribing to *Writer's Digest*, which offers valuable information on how to get into the business. Another helpful tool is *Writer's Market*, a book that lists the names and addresses of publishers alphabetically and by the subject matter they publish. It was through *Writer's Market* that I found the publisher for this book.

Free-Lancing and Starting a Business

"Being a free-lance paralegal is the culmination of whatever legal talent I have. My income exceeds any salary I could ever earn as an employee of a law firm," says Linda Harrington, president of Linda Harrington Associates in San Francisco. "The free-lance aspect of our profession is growing. I hear of paralegals in many cities setting up their own businesses. When the attorneys realize the economic benefits to them, free-lancing will be an arrangement suggested by them, not merely accepted by them."

Ms. Harrington is one of the paralegal profession's success stories. She spent over seven years in several different law firms gaining experience in the areas of probate, bankruptcy, civil litigation, domestic relations, and personal injury law. In 1973, she decided to strike out on her own and began her business by offering free-lance probate services from her house with the aid of an answering service and typewriter. Quite an accomplishment if you consider that during the early 1970s many lawyers had never even heard of a paralegal, let alone a free-lance paralegal. Today Ms. Harrington employs three paralegals, a file clerk, and a secretary. The services offered by her company include the preparation of tax returns, accountings, inventories, and other court documents. All of the work performed by her staff is reviewed by attorneys.

She has some sound advice about free-lancing: "Choose an area where there's money to be made. For example, personal injury is not a good specialty area because most lawyers work on contingency. On the other hand, the probate area is almost guaranteed money because there isn't a winner or loser. Your fee is based on a percentage of the estate. What scares me the most are the people who come out of paralegal programs and have never worked in a law firm environment. Their main reason for becoming a paralegal is to start their own business. When they get out there, they realize they do not have the experience; they're not prepared."

Not all free-lance paralegals operate businesses like Linda Harrington Associates. Many are sole proprietors who work out of their home and make just enough money to live on.

How to start a free-lance paralegal business. For each paralegal, the path to free-lancing is slightly different. Linda Harrington began to free-lance while working as a full-time paralegal. I began free-lancing for the company I had been working at when it announced plans to relocate farther away than I wanted to commute. After quitting as a full-time employee, I contracted for several months with the legal department until the relocation was complete. Other free-lance assignments came to me by word of mouth.

At some point in our careers, most of us dream of owning our own business. In the early 1980s, it seemed like everyone wanted to be an entrepreneur. But as we all know, it's easier said than done. According to the Small Business Administration, 90 percent of all businesses fail within the first three years, which is not an encouraging statistic. Before you decide to strike out on your own, consider the following.

1. *Don't quit your present position.* The safest and most conservative approach is to do work on the side while retaining your full-time position. When the extra work begins to interfere with your full-time job, it may be time to devote all your efforts to your new business.

2. *Cultivate your contacts.* Any free-lance paralegal will tell you that networking and word-of-mouth referrals are vital to a successful business. Local paralegal and attorney associations are excellent places to advertise your services.

3. *Sell a specialty.* Part of Linda Harrington's success is due to her expertise in a particular practice area. In addition to probate, other promising free-lance areas include litigation, computerized litigation support services, and corporate law. Litigation and computerized litigation support are probably the most popular services offered by free-lancers. Typical jobs include summarizing depositions, preparing for trial, drafting pleadings, interviewing clients, cite checking, locating witnesses, researching facts, and managing computerized litigation support systems. A paralegal with experience in corporate law could offer incorporation services.

4. *Minimize your start-up costs.* Should you rent office space or could you start the business out of your home? If you decide to work out of an office, don't go out and purchase the most expensive office furniture, computer, or phone systems. This is a common mistake. Keep overhead to a minimum and it will be easier to show a profit.

Independent contractor or employee. A question that has come up in my own experience as a free-lance paralegal is whether I was an independent contractor or an employee. The answer has important ramifications for both the paralegal and the employer.

147

As an independent contractor, you're allowed to operate as a sole proprietor and take certain business deductions on state and federal income taxes. Employees can't take those deductions.

One of the most important guidelines for determining the difference between an independent contractor and an employee involves the issue of who controls the work performed. An independent contractual relationship can be assumed when an employer receives the final product and is not involved in the methods used to perform the work. This is a difficult criterion to meet for paralegals whose job by definition entails performing work under the supervision of an attorney. However, experienced paralegals will tell you that the phrase "under the supervision of an attorney" is loosely followed—attorneys don't always have the time to review a paralegal's work.

Free-lance versus independent paralegal. It's important to understand the distinction between an independent paralegal and a free-lance paralegal. Independent paralegal is a title coined by Ralph Warner, cofounder of Nolo Press and the self-help law movement, to describe a nonlawyer who offers services directly to the public and does not work under the supervision of an attorney. As I said earlier, most states consider this a crime—unauthorized practice of law. A free-lancer is someone who offers services to attorneys and works under their supervision.

Pursuing Additional Education

This is a traditional method for switching careers and one that should be considered by paralegals, but it's difficult because it often involves a combination of putting out extra energy, giving up time, and juggling finances.

Law school. A discussion of career alternatives wouldn't be complete without mentioning the so-called road to riches—law school. There are many misconceptions surrounding law school. My experiences have led me to discover that:

- Contrary to popular belief, attending law school does not automatically mean you'll earn a six-figure income. Also, not every attorney who works for a law firm becomes a partner.
- Unlike other graduate degree programs that weigh work background and personal experiences for admission, law schools place a great deal of emphasis on two figures: undergraduate grade point average and Law School Admission Test (LSAT) scores. If your GPA is average and/or if you are

not a good test taker, getting into a good law school will be difficult.

- Most law firms, no matter how large or small, want the best lawyers. Therefore, most recruit the top law students from the top schools in the country.
- Only the top law school graduates will receive starting salaries of $60,000 to $75,000 per year.
- Many experienced paralegals earn just as much as lawyers who have graduated from less competitive law schools.
- Many people attend law school because they just don't know what else to do. That's the wrong reason to become a lawyer.
- In weak moments, some lawyers will admit that practicing law is not what they thought it would be.
- Paralegals are probably the most qualified individuals to make a decision about attending law school.

From what I've seen, I sincerely believe there are easier ways to make a living than being a lawyer. An attorney I worked for once remarked, "If I had to do it over again I'd become either an investment banker or an orthodontist—less work for more money."

If you're considering law school, you might want to read Ralph Warner's *29 Reasons Not to Go to Law School.* As he puts it, "This book can save you three years, $30,000, and your sanity."

There are, however, two sides to every coin. Mary Hitt is an attorney with Thorp, Reed & Armstrong in Pittsburgh, Pennsylvania. She was a paralegal for many years and a president of the NFPA before she decided to become an attorney. "I was a tax paralegal for a long time and was very involved in the field," she says. "I did everything I could to advance myself as a paralegal. I received a master's degree in tax and was an enrolled IRS agent, which allowed me to represent clients at IRS and administrative hearings. However, after all these things I still wasn't getting the responsibility I wanted. Instead they gave the work to a recent law school graduate who clearly didn't know half of what I knew. I finally realized that if I wanted to assume more responsibility, I had to go and get the piece of paper. In my first year of law school I learned a lot I didn't know. I came to understand why attorneys think the way they do. But after two years, I thought there was no way that I need three years of law school to do the work.

"The major difference between being a paralegal and an attorney is that attorneys have a lot more responsibility. You are actually making the decision for the client and interpreting the law. You get the hassles and you get the rewards."

The question you have to ask yourself when considering a law degree is how much responsibility you want out of a job and career. Clearly, Mary went to law school for the right reasons. She hit the limit of her responsibilities as a paralegal but was interested enough in the area to want to assume a higher level of responsibility.

Another alternative, of course, would be to attend law school to obtain a degree but not pursue a career as a lawyer. I know someone who didn't pass the California bar (actually I know many people who didn't pass the bar) and is now selling commercial real estate. The only reason he was hired was that he had a J.D.

Other education alternatives. One of the first attorneys I worked for advised me to get an M.B.A. and not bother with a law degree because, according to him, "You can do more with an M.B.A." An M.B.A. was to the 1980s what a law degree was to the 1970s. It seemed everyone was getting an M.B.A. and heading for Wall Street. Then came the October 1987 stock market crash and the insider-trading scandals. Jobs were lost and the M.B.A. was seen in a more realistic light.

For paralegals interested in moving into management, an M.B.A. is still a good bet. You don't have to go to the best business school in the country to get a great job. In addition, you can attend business school at night while working full-time. Just try to do this with law school—I know someone who did, and she has yet to recover from the experience.

Besides an M.B.A., there are other education alternatives to pursue. For instance, a tax paralegal might do course work in accounting to earn a CPA license. Corporate and securities paralegals could take courses to earn a certified financial planner (CFP) license. By the same token, a real estate paralegal might want to obtain a real estate license.

No matter which option you choose—from staying in your present position to pursuing additional education—you need to take an active role in shaping your career. Opportunity comes in many disguises.

The next chapter discusses licensing, certification, and other issues that are critical to the future of the paralegal profession. Because these matters will affect every paralegal's job, they are too important—and too controversial—to be ignored.

Chapter

10

Licensing, Certification, and Other Cutting-Edge Issues

The world hates change, yet it is the only thing that has brought progress.

Charles F. Kettering

In 1972, Rosemary Furman, a court reporter in Jacksonville, Florida, opened a legal typing business, the Northside Secretarial Service. For a modest fee, she typed divorce, name change, adoption, and bankruptcy forms. She didn't give legal advice—her clients made their own decisions about those matters—and she required customers to sign a disclaimer stating that they knew she wasn't a lawyer. Five years later, the Florida Bar Association charged her with practicing law without a license and claimed that the public wasn't aware of how many complaints it had received about her from her clients. In 1979, the state's supreme court found Ms. Furman guilty and sentenced her to four months in jail. Her appeal was turned down by the U.S. Supreme Court in 1984, but the governor of Florida commuted the sentence the day before it was supposed to begin in exchange for her promise that she would shut down her business permanently.

This famous case illustrates one of the most controversial issues facing paralegals today—nonlawyers practicing law without a license.

If you're contemplating a career as a paralegal, it's important to understand this and other issues that concern the profession—including certification, education standards, and the status of paralegals as nonexempt employees under U.S. labor laws. The existence of these issues makes it apparent that it's time to reassess the roles of attorneys and paralegals in terms of the legal industry's goal to make high-quality, cost-effective legal services available to every American citizen. This kind of reassessment will also help the paralegal profession achieve its own goal of broadening paralegal job responsibilities.

Issue: Unauthorized Practice of Law

The statutes, court rules, and bar association powers that prohibit nonlawyers from providing legal services directly to the public are called the unauthorized practice laws (UPL). Believe it or not, these laws are so vague and ambiguous, they provide very little guidance. The bottom line is that there is no uniform definition of just what *does* constitute the practice of law.

The existence of the UPL raises some hotly debated questions. Why should lawyers have a monopoly on every aspect of the delivery of legal services—including the right to fill in the blanks on preprinted divorce forms? What's wrong with nonlawyers providing routine and basic legal services directly to the public? Why can't we have several different levels of legal professionals who could offer varying degrees of legal services at competitive rates?

Defining the Problem

The issue of unauthorized practice of law revolves around two separate concerns: (1) the inability of the legal profession to provide all citizens access to high-quality, cost-effective legal services and (2) the difficulty of redefining and expanding the roles and responsibilities of paralegals.

Access to legal services. In 1975, then-president of the American Bar Association James D. Fellers described the bar's most important mission as beginning a push to "bring legal assistance to every American, not just those privileged enough to be able to pay for it or those impoverished enough to be eligible for free legal aid." Fellers put his finger on a basic problem in our society: middle-income people who need basic legal services for divorces, incorporations, name changes, wills, adoptions, or bankruptcy are not rich enough to pay for high-priced attorneys and not poor enough to be eligible for legal aid.

The legal industry responded to this prodding by introducing prepaid legal insurance plans, group legal services, and lawyer referral services; lifting prohibitions on advertising by lawyers; and hiring more paralegals and making better use of them. But many paralegal and consumer groups, and some attorneys, believe that more needs to be done. Looking for ways to lower the cost of basic legal services, these groups believe that properly educated and trained nonlawyers can provide basic services at lower rates than licensed attorneys.

Among the people who object to this solution are lawyers who work as sole practitioners or in small law firms. This segment of lawyers represents over half of all attorneys in private practice and has the most to lose from direct competition with nonlawyers. Attorneys who work in large firms don't have as much to lose. Large firms are busy making money from complex legal transactions and not from simple wills, incorporations, or bankruptcies.

Perhaps now you can begin to see the dilemma. Lawyers are ethically bound to provide all citizens access to legal services, but because of the cost of those services, not all citizens can afford a lawyer when they need one. One solution—the use of trained nonlawyers who could provide basic legal services at lower rates than licensed lawyers—is objected to by a large number of lawyers who see it as a competitive threat. The legal industry's response has been to concentrate on methods of providing cost-effective services that don't involve nonlawyers.

Expanding paralegal roles. Recent challenges to UPL have come from paralegals who are involved in the profession's struggle to redefine itself and from citizen groups that want greater access to the legal system. Unauthorized practice laws affect paralegals by limiting the scope of their responsibilities and preventing them from offering services directly to the public. A relaxation of UPL would mean that paralegals could expand their role and that new areas for employment would open up.

Similar scenarios for medical paraprofessionals. Paralegals are not the only ones challenging occupational laws. Faced with similar issues, nurses, midwives, podiatrists, and psychologists are among the medical paraprofessionals clamoring for the right to provide certain types of care—such as giving examinations, prescribing medication, and performing certain surgeries—currently restricted to physicians.

In 1983, Missouri's supreme court ruled that two nurses at family planning clinics were not practicing medicine without a license by giving breast and pelvic examinations and dispensing contraceptives. In its decision, the court specified the growing need for "broadening of the field of practice by the nursing profession" as justification for its ruling. On the other hand, two nurses in Nashville, Tennessee, were denied staff privileges at local hospitals and had their malpractice insurance canceled by its physician-owned insurance company when they tried to open a private midwifery practice.

Examples of paraprofessionals trying to push back restrictions on what they can and can't do include optometrists (who don't have medical degrees) who are challenging ophthalmologists (who have medical degrees) by seeking the authority to use drugs to treat glaucoma, and dental hygienists who are fighting for the authority to clean teeth outside dentist offices. Interestingly, podiatrists in California recently won an eight-year battle with orthopedic surgeons for the right to perform ankle surgery (they had previously been restricted to foot surgery).

The physicians who are being challenged argue that their opposition to expanded paraprofessional responsibilities has more to do with the potential decrease in the quality of services than the increase in competition. Some attorneys use the same argument against the challenges of nonlawyers.

On the flip side, most paraprofessionals don't consider themselves in competition with professionals who are educated and trained to perform complex services and procedures. They view themselves as providers of basic services at lower costs. I don't know many paralegals who would want to be responsible for a complicated legal transaction, but I know quite a few who could correctly prepare a simple incorporation at a much lower cost than an attorney.

The Debate over Licensure

Nearly everyone agrees that something must be done to provide cost-effective legal services to all citizens. Most attorneys and paralegals also agree that nonlawyers should play a greater role in the delivery of legal services; they just don't agree on the extent of that role. Should nonlawyers be allowed to provide certain services directly to the public without the supervision of an attorney? If so, should they be licensed or regulated in some way? If they are licensed, what form should it take? There are five distinct viewpoints on this issue that you should understand. In order for you to understand them, a definition of licensing will be helpful.

Licensing is defined as a form of regulation by which a government agency grants the right to engage in a certain occupation and use a particular title to people who meet predetermined qualifications—passing an approved educational program and/or qualifying exams, for instance.

No licensing and no independent paralegals. The most conservative position belongs to the ABA's General Practice Section. It is opposed to licensing of any kind for paralegals and believes paralegals should always work under the supervision of attorneys. Speaking out against a recommendation for limited licensing made by the ABA's Commission on Professionalism, the General Practice Section stated:

> *In an era of significant lawyer unemployment and underemployment, it makes no sense to turn the practice of law over to unsupervised paralegals, however limited their license may be. The cost-effective use of paralegals should be encouraged, but supervision by a law-school-trained attorney is the key to proper legal representation, not a "limited" license.*

The ABA's Standing Committee on Legal Assistants has a similar opinion. As you recall from Chapter 1, the committee has been extensively involved since 1968 in the development of the paralegal field. Its position since 1975 has been that licensing would offer no benefits to the paralegal profession, legal profession, or general public. It believes that the public is already protected by the licensed attorneys through whom paralegals work and, ultimately, that it is the responsibility of attorneys to protect the public. It reaffirmed this stance in 1985.

The NALA position also falls into this category. The NALA definition of legal assistants refers only to individuals who work under the supervision of attorneys, including free-lance legal assistants who contract their services to law firms. The NALA never uses the term paralegal, and its definition does not include independent paralegals. As with the standing committee's position, the NALA believes that it is the attorney who is responsible for the legal assistant's work and who is ultimately responsible to the public. Since the process of licensing is the regulation of a profession by government to protect the public's health, safety, and welfare, the NALA doesn't support licensure for legal assistants. According to the NALA definition of legal assistants, licensing isn't necessary because the public is protected by attorney licenses.

Independent paralegals are okay, but licensing is necessary. The ABA Commission on Professionalism released a report in 1986 (referred to above) that recommended limited licensing of paralegals so that they could perform certain basic legal services independently. Chiding the legal industry for its no-license stance, the commission stated:

> *[I]t can no longer be claimed that lawyers have the exclusive possession of the esoteric knowledge required and are therefore the only ones able to advise clients on any matter concerning the law. Inroads on lawyer exclusivity have been made and will continue to be made. Lawyer resistance to such inroads for selfish reasons only brings discredit on the profession.*

The report encouraged direct nonlawyer competition with lawyers. (It's not surprising that the general practice division suggested the commentary be reversed.)

Another opinion that favors limited licensing belongs to past president of the California state bar Terry Anderlini. As part of a panel on UPL sponsored by the San Francisco Association of Legal Assistants in 1988, Mr. Anderlini said that regulating nonlawyers through training, testing, and continuing education would raise the standard of legal services. He suggested that a regulatory body composed of attorneys, consumers, and nonlawyers be set up to oversee the licensure of nonlawyers. Anderlini also expressed belief that the marketplace will demonstrate the need for different levels of service and expertise and said that attorneys should not view nonlawyers who provide legal services as a competitive threat.

Unfortunately, those who do agree that licensing is necessary don't agree on what form it should take. Should it be voluntary or mandatory? Should there be continuing education requirements? Should the guidelines be formal or informal? Should there be enforceable contracts between the consumer and the nonlawyer? Should nonlawyers be required to register with various federal and state agencies? Should there be bar requirements? The list is endless.

No licensing, but independent paralegals are okay. The NFPA advocates the concept of nonlawyers, but it's opposed to any form of regulation or licensing that might limit the growth of the paralegal profession at this time. It believes that the profession hasn't yet developed to the point where licensing would be a benefit and that before any decision on licensing is made industry-wide, a survey to study competencies for job performance and to establish minimum entrance requirements and course curriculum standards for paralegal education programs should be conducted and analyzed.

The NFPA definition of paralegals is quite broad and includes paralegals who work under the supervision of attorneys as well as independent paralegals.

Let legal technicians deliver legal services. The latest wrinkle in the unauthorized practice of law debate comes from California. The Public Protection Committee (PPC) of the California state bar was created to identify areas in which nonlawyers called legal technicians could provide legal services to the public and to develop standards for nonlawyer regulation. After sponsoring public hearings throughout the state in 1988, the PPC proposed that California drop most of its restrictions on the practice of law by nonlawyers. It recommended:

1. Replacing traditional unauthorized practice laws with legislation prohibiting nonlawyers from claiming to be lawyers.
2. Protecting consumers from fraud by requiring nonlawyer registration (as opposed to licensing) and requiring nonlawyers to inform their clients that they are not attorneys.
3. Establishing civil and criminal remedies for nonfeasance (the failure to do what needed to be done) and misfeasance (the performance of a lawful action in an illegal or improper way). Both nonfeasance and misfeasance can result in charges of malpractice or negligence.

The California bar's Board of Governors approved a watered-down version of the recommendations in August 1989 and called for further study of the concept of legal technicians. The resolution did not specifically state whether the occupation of legal technician should be permitted to exist and did not address the question of who should regulate nonlawyers. As a consequence, it's still too early to tell whether there will be an expanded role for nonlawyers and paralegals in California.

Deregulate the entire legal industry. This controversial opinion isn't held by very many people within the industry, but there are several consumer and some legal organizations that champion the idea. W. Clark Durant III, an attorney and former chairman of the Legal Services Corporation, has become a leading advocate.

Addressing an ABA meeting in 1987, Durant suggested that *all* unauthorized practice laws be repealed and bar admissions be deregulated (an unprecedented recommendation for an attorney!). Durant emphasized that the two barriers to making low-cost legal services widely available are the UPL and restrictions on how one becomes a lawyer. He believes that deregulation would effectively eliminate those barriers.

The most frequently cited argument for deregulation is that the poor, especially poor members of minority groups, deserve increased representation in the legal system and greater access to high-quality affordable legal services. In Durant's view, however:

> *Representation of the poor is not the primary root of the crisis. The problems are far broader and hence the scope of reform must be far broader.*

Durant is not alone in his position. As mentioned in Chapter 1, in 1971, Ralph Warner and Nolo Press cofounder Charles Sherman also cofounded the WAVE Project, one of the first nonlawyer divorce form preparation services. The project gave birth to the self-help law movement, the underlying principle of which is that with some guidance and practical assistance, consumers can handle many legal matters on their own. It relies heavily on self-help law books and software for the preparation of wills, divorce papers, bankruptcies, and incorporations, among many other basic legal services, and the concept of independent paralegals to help consumers complete legal forms. In the past two decades, the WAVE Project has helped consumers on the West Coast save thousands of dollars in legal fees.

In the Winter 1987 issue of *Nolo News,* Mr. Warner and Nolo Press publisher and attorney Steve Elias made a plea for deregulation. They suggested that the most realistic way to determine the level of expertise needed for a particular service is to focus on the work that needs to be done, not on the person who would do it. They suggested using the following criteria for making the determination: whether the case is contested or uncontested, whether academic training or hands-on experience is called for, and what the liability would be if a mistake were made. They believe that these criteria suggest a place for different levels of legal services and that people other than attorneys can be qualified to deliver certain types of legal services.

Perhaps the most common working example of the Nolo concept is the preparation of income tax forms. Citizens can opt to use a tax attorney, a CPA, or a tax specialist (such as H&R Block), or they can do their taxes themselves. In Nolo's view, this system can be applied to certain legal services—divorce, for instance. A divorce is either uncontested (simple) or contested (involved). Depending on the complexity of the divorce, the consumer would be able to choose from several types of services. (Under our current system, lawyers must be involved in even the simplest divorces.)

Another organization that advocates deregulation is Help Abolish Legal Tyranny (HALT), a national nonpartisan public interest group of more than 150,000 members. In April 1988, HALT sponsored a conference entitled The Next Decade: A Revolution in Legal

Services. Those gathered for it concluded that in order for all consumers to have access to our legal system, the entire system needs to be overhauled and nonlawyers allowed to deliver certain legal services. The conference members also concluded that before nonlawyer delivery of services becomes a reality, some form of nonlawyer regulation is necessary.

Issue: Certification

Less controversial than the issue of unauthorized practice of law, but one that has been debated since the early 1970s, is the issue of paralegal certification. It's less controversial because it's a voluntary designation and because there's less at stake for lawyers—after all, certification poses no threat to their livelihood. According to a survey of lawyers conducted by the ABA Standing Committee on Legal Assistants in 1984, over 51 percent of those who responded felt there was a need for paralegal certification, while only 10 percent felt there was a need for paralegal licensure.

By definition, certification is a voluntary form of regulation through which a nongovernmental agency or association recognizes an individual who has met certain predetermined qualifications. Such qualifications include graduation from an accredited program, acceptable performance on qualifying examinations, and completion of a given amount of work experience.

Arguments for Certification

Proponents believe that certification provides standards for a certain level of paralegal proficiency, aids employers in the selection of prospective employees, and improves the status of the profession. They also believe that it helps to verify the completion of minimal education requirements and to reassure consumers of a paralegal's competency.

Among the major advocates of certification is the NALA. When it incorporated in 1975, one of its top priorities was to develop standards for the field. After conducting a study, it developed the first and (still) only national voluntary legal assistant certification program in the country. The purpose of the CLA program, as mentioned in Chapter 6, was to establish a national standard of excellence and achievement, develop a means of identifying individuals who meet those standards, and bring professional recognition to the occupation by emphasizing that it's a learned profession. The CLA designation is also intended to deter people without the proper training and work experience from calling themselves legal assistants.

The program awards the CLA designation to paralegals only after they have met certain eligibility requirements and passed a qualifying exam. More than 2,700 paralegals have received the designation since 1976, and nearly 200 have received specialty certification. The NALA sees the designation as a mark of distinction and believes it has been established over the years as a means of recognizing paralegals who have met certain standards and attained a certain level of achievement.

In the past decade, several states have shown an interest in paralegal certification. Florida Legal Assistants, Inc., has had a voluntary certification exam since 1982. In 1986, the Legal Assistants Division of the Texas State Bar Association studied several proposals for certifying paralegals. While public hearings were held, comments were mixed. A certification proposal was defeated in July 1988. Washington State recently instituted a paraprofessional licensing program, but very few paralegals have participated so far. Interestingly, Oregon established the country's first bar-sponsored certification program in 1974, but it was disbanded six years later because it was perceived as inhibiting the growth of the profession.

Arguments Against Certification

Surprisingly, not all paralegals and lawyers agree about the benefits of certification. The NFPA's position is similar to its stance on licensing. This position dates back to 1975, when it was determined that it was necessary and advisable for paralegals to retain control over the creation of standards and guidelines for the development of the profession. A task force on the issue of certification concluded in 1985 that the best way to advance the profession would be to develop methods for educating paralegals, attorneys, educators, and the general public about what paralegals do—not by developing standards for certification and licensing.

Through various forums, lawyers have also participated in the debate. In 1975, the ABA Standing Committee on Legal Assistants conducted hearings throughout the country to discuss the issue of certification. At that time, the committee concluded that certification, licensure, and regulation of any kind would restrict the growth and development of the field and were, therefore, premature. It revisited the issue in 1985 and concluded that the benefits gained from certifying minimal paralegal competency don't outweigh the time, effort, and expense necessary to implement such programs. The committee found that any certification of advanced paralegal proficiency in specialized areas of law should be under the supervision of a board that includes lawyers, paralegals, educators, and members of the general public.

Issue: Paralegal Education

It has been suggested by professionals outside of the legal industry that education, not regulation (in the form of licensing or certification), is the key to professionalism within most occupations. But for the paralegal profession, this is easier said than done.

The quality of paralegal education is an ongoing concern of paralegals, educators, attorneys, and employers. As mentioned in Chapter 6, unlike professions that adhere to strict educational standards, the paralegal field is still open to individuals with a wide variety of backgrounds. In addition, paralegal education can range from three-month certificate programs to four-year bachelor's degree programs and everything in-between. At this time the only standard in paralegal education is whether or not a program is approved by the ABA.

The ABA Standing Committee on Legal Assistants believes that the best means of increasing the proficiency and quality of paralegals is to increase the number of ABA-approved training programs and the number of continuing education programs.

Both the NFPA and the NALA appear to be in agreement when it comes to the issue of paralegal education. Both associations work directly with the ABA approval commission. But while everyone involved seems to agree that educational standards for paralegals need to be developed, as stated in Chapter 6, guidelines have yet to be adopted industry-wide.

Some progress has been made on that front. In an event that first took place in March 1988, called The Conclave, representatives from various paralegal, attorney, and educational associations met to discuss, among other things, paralegal education. In the report that followed, all groups agreed that:

- There is a substantial amount of diversity in the types of paralegal training offered and in the educational backgrounds of students.
- There are difficulties in teaching because of the lack of standardized textbooks and methods of instruction.

- The information available to employers regarding the quality of paralegal training programs that would enable them to make informed hiring decisions is insufficient.
- There is a trend toward hiring entry-level paralegals with bachelor's degrees.
- The general education requirements within paralegal training programs serve to eliminate the disparity between the diverse educational backgrounds of students.
- The minimum of 15 hours of legal specialty courses currently required by the ABA guidelines is too low.
- A campaign to educate attorneys on high-quality paralegal education should be instituted by the ABA, state and local bar associations, and paralegal associations.

Some of the other significant recommendations made in this report focused on changes in curriculum design. The report stated that a minimum of 30 units of general education be required and include courses in computers, math or accounting, history, government, and communication and focus on analytical and quantitative skills. In addition, the report recommended that factual and legal research, legal ethics, the American legal system, and the professional legal environment be included in legal specialty course requirements. The report also emphasized that internships should be a part of every paralegal training program.

The recommendations of The Conclave represent a step toward the development of standards in paralegal education, but perhaps most significant is the communication that the meeting fostered between the various groups. While the issue of paralegal education is far from being resolved, it's safe to assume that education requirements are likely to become more rigorous.

Issue: Exempt or Nonexempt?

Should paralegals be compensated for overtime? According to current U.S. Department of Labor rulings, paralegals are covered under the wage and hour provisions of the Fair Labor Standards Act of 1938 (FLSA) and are considered nonexempt employees who must receive overtime pay after 40 hours of work in one week. This has created quite a stir. So what's the problem? Under the FLSA, exempt employees are those who are employed in bona fide executive, administrative, or professional capacities; exercise a large degree of independent judgment in their jobs; and are relatively free of supervision by others. The labor department believes that problems related to UPL make it impossible for paralegals to meet the independent judgment qualification of exempt employees. The implication of this interpretation is that, in terms of employment law, the paralegal field may not even qualify as a profession.

Paralegals are divided on this issue. Some believe that the exempt classification would enhance their professional status. Others feel that it would give employers a legal way of requiring them to work long hours without paying overtime. Still others believe that there's nothing demeaning or less professional about nonexempt status.

Since the paralegal profession is rapidly changing, it's possible that future studies of the profession by the Department of Labor will recommend that it be given an exempt status. A special committee to review the status of paralegals was established by the department in 1981. Nearly a decade later, it has yet to issue a report.

Encouraging Signs

The growing acceptance of paralegals and their integration into our legal system is evidenced by several recent developments.

Representation Before Administrative Boards

Can paralegals working in law firms appear before administrative courts and represent their firm's clients?

The question has been brewing in California for some time and is closely related to the UPL issue. In February 1989, the California State Bar Association issued an opinion that permits paralegals who work in law firms to represent firm clients before administrative courts. The bar's Standing Committee on Professional Responsibility and Conduct found that adequately supervised paralegals can appear before the Workers' Compensation Appeals Board to file petitions and motions as long as the client consents to the use of a paralegal.

It's true that this action is a far cry from deregulation—the decision applies in only one state and it's limited to workers' compensation cases—but it does signal a loosening of UPL and the expansion of paralegal responsibilities.

ABA Associate Membership

In 1987, the ABA voted to amend its bylaws to create an associate status for paralegals, which allows them to participate in many ABA activities.

The ABA believes this will further its efforts to ensure that the public receives effective, affordable legal services. The ABA encourages all paralegals to take advantage of associate status in order to enhance their working relationships with attorneys. The NFPA does not support the action. The NFPA's members are concerned with the underlying implications of associate status. They believe that the growth and independence of the paralegal profession is compromised when viewed as a subprofession. The NALA supported the ABA move.

While this is by no means an earth-shattering development, it does signal an effort toward greater communication between paralegals and attorneys.

Legislative Efforts

Should paralegal services that are performed under the supervision of an attorney be considered when setting fees in certain probate cases? According to Bruce D. Sires, a tax and probate attorney, the answer is "yes." On January 1, 1988, a law that allows compensation for paralegal services performed in probate, guardianship, and conservatorship proceedings went into effect in California. According to an article in the *Los Angeles Daily Journal*, Sires was instrumental in getting the bill through the state legislature. Besides paralegals benefiting from the law, Sires believes the public will benefit by realizing the cost savings of using paralegals.

Malpractice Insurance

"The first malpractice suit against a legal assistant is inevitable," said H. Jeffrey Valentine, the National Paralegal Association (NPA) executive director, in the December 2, 1988, edition of the *New York Times*. "It will send shock waves through the entire paralegal community, but the independents will have the most to fear." As such, the NPA is planning to offer malpractice insurance (for $50 per year compared to the $2,000 attorneys usually pay) in the near future.

The availability of such insurance further illustrates the growing status of the profession.

Legal Technicians

Let's not forget the August 1989 resolution by the California state bar mentioned earlier in this chapter. The resolution fell short of expectations, but the idea that a bar association is even considering the issue of licensure is a big leap forward for paralegals.

Clearly, all the issues mentioned in this chapter will continue to be debated for some time—particularly the issue of licensing non-lawyers and paralegals. Perhaps in the not-too-distant future, the goal of providing all citizens access to affordable legal services and the ability of paralegals to open their own legal services business will become a reality. I believe the best is still to come for this twenty-year-old profession.

Afterword
The Future for Paralegals

Minds are like parachutes — they only function when open.

Thomas Dewar

The future holds great promise for the paralegal profession. As consumers continue to demand affordable legal services, paralegals will play an important role in alleviating the burden of high fees. Just what that role will be, however, remains to be seen.

Will paralegals continue to work for attorneys, or will they evolve into professionals with the ability to offer basic legal services directly to the public? If so, will their authorization to practice law involve licensing or certification, or will formal paralegal education and training be enough? Does our legal system have room for two levels of professionals, or will it continue to be dominated by lawyers?

One thing is certain. Paralegals represent change, and change is almost always met with resistance — particularly from those who benefit from the status quo. It is this sense of change — being part of a profession that's still evolving, still striving to overcome resistance, and still trying to define itself — that I find one of the most interesting aspects of the occupation.

Future Trends

For those who become paralegals in the 1990s, a paralegal career will be exciting and challenging. The challenges come from a more complex legal environment — a result of lawyers being forced to examine their profession in new ways. Increased competition for clients, specialization, greater use of technology and computers, the advent of advertising and marketing, and the emergence of alternative dispute resolution methods have transformed the legal industry and affected the responsibilities of paralegals and will continue to do both into the next decade. Though predicting the future is risky, I believe, as many industry watchers do, that the following trends will surface in the years ahead.

- Greater emphasis will be placed on education. More employers will require a bachelor's degree or a paralegal certificate or both. With an increasing pool of available paralegal graduates, it will be more difficult to enter the field without a formal paralegal education.

- More sophisticated and substantive legal work will be performed by paralegals. Attorneys and other employers of paralegals will continue to learn what paralegals are capable of doing.

- Recognition of the paralegal profession by the general public will continue to increase. Clients and consumers of legal services will become more aware of the benefits of using paralegals to reduce legal fees. More non-law-related employers will realize that paralegal skills and knowledge can be useful in their areas of business. As a result, the career will continue to gain in popularity.

- Increased recognition of the profession will result in new career alternatives with the potential for greater compensation for individuals with paralegal skills and experience.

- More paralegals will start their own businesses. This will occur as a result of corporate downsizing and the desire of paralegals for a more flexible work environment.

- Competition for paralegal jobs will increase dramatically as more individuals discover the field. Although the Department of Labor estimates that over 62,000 paralegal jobs will be created in the 1990s, to be competitive, individuals entering the field will require more knowledge, skills, and training than their predecessors did.

- Paralegals will be required to be computer literate. Computers are here to stay and will continue to invade every aspect of our lives (as well as every law firm in the country).

- Paralegals will have the opportunity to become experts in particular legal areas as the practice of law becomes more specialized. This will result in greater job satisfaction and increased compensation.

- Licensing and certification will continue to be hotly debated issues. Since paralegals can't agree on a solution themselves, it's unlikely that these issues will be settled in the near future.

- A new breed of paralegal—one who chooses the profession by design rather than by accident—will emerge.

Expanding Job Responsibilities

I believe that there will be a major expansion of paralegal roles and job responsibilities over the next decade. In fact, a 1989 study entitled Survey of Non-Traditional Paralegal Responsibilities, conducted by the NFPA Committee on the Expansion of Paralegal Responsibilities, identified some of the new and nontraditional directions paralegals are already moving in.

The committee asked "traditional" paralegals to respond to a questionnaire about the nontraditional tasks and responsibilities that they performed. (Traditional paralegals were defined as paralegals who work for attorneys in law firms as opposed to "independent" paralegals, who do not.) The 274 paralegals who responded confirmed what had been suspected all along—more paralegals work in areas that were once the exclusive domain of attorneys. Some of the findings are shown in the following chart.

Survey of Nontraditional Paralegal Tasks and Responsibilities
(1989 NFPA Study)

Tasks/Responsibilities	Percent Performing
Recommend client action	75+ (40% on a regular basis)
Conduct client interviews without attorney present	75
Decide whether or not to accept new clients	30
Handle probate matters directly with a client independent of an attorney	25
Prepare court documents and send them to client before review by a supervising attorney	25
Attend depositions without a supervising attorney present and ask questions at depositions	25
Initiate settlement discussions on behalf of client	23

(continued)

Survey of Nontraditional Paralegal Tasks and Responsibilities
(continued)

Tasks/Responsibilities	Percent Performing
Recommend client action	75+ (40% on a regular basis)
Advise client on ramifications of a settlement without a supervising attorney present	22
Attend and conduct real estate closings without a supervising attorney present	≈ 20
Appear at settlement conferences without an attorney present	15
Have authority to make, refuse, or accept a settlement offer on behalf of client without attorney consultation	12
Appear at trial-setting conferences without an attorney	11
Conclude case by settlement, judgment, or other method without attorney intervention	10
Negotiate fee agreements with clients	9
Represent clients who are being deposed	6
Have a fee-splitting arrangement with an attorney	5

While this study doesn't represent all paralegals, the findings support the idea that even paralegals who work in the most traditional settings perform tasks that at one time were considered "practicing law." Although some of the percentages seem small, they are significant in that they represent what inevitably will be future components of paralegal job responsibilities.

A Final Word

As the paralegal profession matures, the lines between attorney and paralegal will blur even more, and the inevitable conflict between the old and the new will continue. Such conflict was predicted in another context by Alvin Toffler over a decade ago in *The Third Wave.*

In his bestselling book, Toffler, a futurist, examined the major waves of change that affect social, economic, and cultural systems worldwide. The First Wave of change was the agricultural revolution. It was overtaken by the Second Wave—the industrial revolution. Toffler predicts that the Third Wave, the postindustrial era that we are now in, will sweep aside many of the changes introduced in the Second Wave. Toffler writes, "the unevadable fact remains that the Third Wave production in the office, as it collides with the old Second Wave systems, will produce anxiety and conflict as well as reorganization, restructuring, and—for some—rebirth into new careers and opportunities."

I believe the paralegal profession fits in well with Toffler's prediction. Change is opportunity. And many opportunities lie ahead for paralegals.

Associations

Paralegal Associations

California Association of Freelance Paralegals (CAFP)
P.O. Box 3267
Berkeley, CA 94703
213-251-3826

Founded in 1988 to provide and assist free-lance paralegals with information and resources specific to free-lancing. The association publishes a newsletter entitled Freelancer *six times per year.*

National Association of Legal Assistants (NALA)
1601 South Main, Suite 300
Tulsa, OK 74119
918-587-6828

Membership in the NALA is open to individual paralegals and paralegal associations. The NALA publishes a bimonthly newsletter called Facts and Findings *and offers the only certified legal assistant designation in the country. Contact the NALA for a list of member paralegal associations in your area.*

National Federation of Paralegal Associations (NFPA)
104 Wilmot Road, Suite 201
Deerfield, IL 60015-5195
312-940-8800

The NFPA is composed of over forty state and local independent paralegal associations. It publishes a quarterly newsletter called the National Paralegal Reporter. *If your local paralegal association is a member of the NFPA, you automatically receive the* National Paralegal Reporter *when you join your local association. Contact the NFPA for a list of member paralegal associations in your area.*

National Paralegal Association (NPA)
P.O. Box 406
Solebury, PA 18963
215-297-8333

Membership is available to individual paralegals and students in paralegal programs. The NPA offers a number of legal and paralegal publications through the Paralegal Book Store. It also publishes a newsletter entitled The Paralegal.

Other Associations

American Association for Paralegal Education (AAfPE)
P.O. Box 40244
Overland Park, KS 66204
913-381-4458

The AAfPE serves paralegal educators and administrators of institutions that offer paralegal training programs. The AAfPE publishes the Journal of Paralegal Education *once a year.*

American Bar Association (ABA)
Standing Committee on Legal Assistants
750 North Lake Shore Drive
Chicago, IL 60611
312-988-5000

Paralegals can join the ABA as associate members. The association publishes Legal Assistants Update *annually, which contains articles on the paralegal profession written by paralegals and attorneys. The ABA also offers other publications relevant to the paralegal profession.*

Association of Legal Administrators (ALA)
104 Wilmot Road, Suite 205
Deerfield, IL 60015-5195
312-940-9240

The ALA's purpose is to enhance the competence and professionalism of the legal administrator and the legal management team. The ALA publishes a journal entitled Legal Administrator.

Legal Assistant Management Association (LAMA)
P.O. Box 40129
Overland Park, KS 66204
913-381-4458

The association disseminates information regarding legal assistant management and promotes the professional standing of legal assistant managers.

Paralegal Training Programs

The following list of paralegal education programs has been developed by the American Bar Association. Although every effort has been made to include all schools that currently offer training programs, some schools may have been overlooked. Programs that are endorsed or accredited by the American Bar Association or the Standing Committee on Legal Assistants are indicated by * (ABA Final Approval) or ** (ABA Provisional Approval).

As the need for program evaluation became apparent, the American Bar Association established appropriate guidelines for institutions to follow when considering establishing a legal assistant program. Thereafter, procedures for obtaining ABA approval of legal assistant programs were developed. Seeking approval of a legal assistant education program from the American Bar Association is a voluntary effort initiated by the institution that offers the program. Nonapproval doesn't necessarily mean that the program being offered is not of good quality.

Alabama

*Auburn University at Montgomery, Department of Justice & Public Safety, Legal Assistant Education, Montgomery, AL 36193

Community College of the Air Force, Maxwell Air Force Base, 745 Selfridge, Maxwell AFB, Montgomery, AL 36113

Faulkner University, Birmingham, 2211 Magnolia Avenue, Birmingham, AL 35205

Faulkner University, Florence, 1001 Florence Boulevard, Florence, AL 35630

Faulkner University, Huntsville, 2650 Jordan Lane, Huntsville, AL 35810

Faulkner University, Mobile, 1050 Government Street, Mobile, AL 36604

Faulkner University, Montgomery, 5345 Atlanta Highway, Montgomery, AL 36193

Huntingdon College, Continuing Education, 1500 East Fairview Avenue, Montgomery, AL 36106

John C. Calhoun State Community College, Paralegal Program, P.O. Box 2216, Decatur, AL 35602-2216

Miles College, Paralegal Studies, P.O. Box 3800, Birmingham, AL 35208

National Academy for Paralegal Studies, Inc., 1572 Montgomery Highway, Suite 100, Birmingham, AL 35216

Northeast Alabama State, Junior College, P.O. Box 159, Rainsville, AL 35986

*Samford University, Division of Paralegal Studies, Birmingham, AL 35229

Southern Institute, Department of Paralegal Studies, 2015 Highland Avenue South, Birmingham, AL 35205

Spring Hill College, Legal Studies Program, Social Science Division, Mobile, AL 36608

University of Alabama at Birmingham, UAB Special Studies, 917 11th Street, South, Birmingham, AL 35294

University of South Alabama, Division of C.E. & Evening Studies, 307 University Boulevard, Mobile, AL 36688

Wallace State Community College, Highway 31, North, Hanceville, AL 35077

Alaska

Alaska Business College, Paralegal Education Department, 800 East Dimond Boulevard, Suite 3-350, Anchorage, AK 99515

Charter College, 4791 Business Park Boulevard, Anchorage, AK 99503

University of Alaska Anchorage, Paralegal Certificate Program, School of Public Affairs–Justice, 3211 Providence Drive, Anchorage, AK 99508

University of Alaska Juneau, Paralegal Studies Program, School of Business, Bill Ray Center, 1108 F Street, Juneau, AK 99801

Arizona

* The American Institute, Paralegal Studies Program, 1300 North Central Avenue, Phoenix, AZ 85004

Apollo College, Legal Assistant Program, 13 West Westmore Road, Tucson, AZ 85705

Arizona State University, Paralegal Program, Department of Administrative Services, Tempe, AZ 85281

Lamson Junior College, 1313 North Second Street, Phoenix, AZ 84004

The Paralegal Institute, 1315 West Indian, School Drawer 33903, Phoenix, AZ 85067

* Phoenix College, Legal Assistant Program, 1201 West Thomas Road, Phoenix, AZ 85013

* Pima Community College, Downtown Campus, 1255 North Stone Avenue, Tucson, AZ 85703

* The Sterling School, Legal Assistant Program, 801 East Indian School Road, Phoenix, AZ 85014

Arkansas

The Institute for Paralegal Training at South Central Career College, 4500 West Commercial Drive, North Little Rock, AR 72116

California

American Paralegal Institute, 21704 Golden Triangle Road, Suite 314, Santa Clarita, CA 91350

American River College, 4700 College Oak Drive, Sacramento, CA 95841

Associated Business Programs, Paralegal Program, 3763 Arlington Avenue, Suite 2, Riverside, CA 92506

Barclay Career Schools, 3460 Wilshire Boulevard, Suite 1111, Los Angeles, CA 90010

Barclay College, Legal Assistant Program, 5172 Orange Avenue, Cypress, CA 90630

California College of Paralegal Studies, 5121 Van Nuys Boulevard, Sherman Oaks, CA 91403

California State University, Chico, Department of Political Science, Paralegal Certificate Program, Chico, CA 95929-0455

California State University, Dominguez Hills, Public Paralegal Certificate Program, School of Social & Behavorial Sciences, Carson, CA 90747

California State University, Hayward, Paralegal Certificate Program, Division of

Extended Education, Hayward, CA 94542

California State University, Los Angeles, Certificate Program for the Legal Assistant, 5151 State University Drive, Los Angeles, CA 90032

California State University, San Bernardino, Paralegal Program, Political Science Department, 5500 University Parkway, San Bernardino, CA 92407

Cañada College, 4200 Farm Hill Boulevard, Redwood City, CA 94061

* Cerritos College, 11110 East Alondra Boulevard, Norwalk, CA 90650

City College of San Francisco, A.A. & Certified Legal Assistant Programs, 50 Phelan Avenue, San Francisco, CA 94112

* Coastline Community College, 11460 Warner Avenue, Fountain Valley, CA 92708

* College of the Sequoias, Paralegal Program, 915 South Mooney Boulevard, Visalia, CA 93227

CSB Plus, Attorney Assistant Certificate Program, Extended Studies & Regional Programs, 9001 Stockdale Highway, Bakersfield, CA 93311-1099

DeAnza College, Legal Assistant Program, 21250 Stevens Creek Boulevard, Cupertino, CA 95014

Dominican College of San Rafael, San Rafael, CA 94901

El Camino College, Legal Assistant Program, 16007 Crenshaw Boulevard, Torrance, CA 90506

Fresno City College, 1101 East University Avenue, Fresno, CA 93741

Humphreys College, 6650 Inglewood Drive, Stockton, CA 92507

Imperial Valley College, P.O. Box 158, Imperial, CA 92251

Lake Tahoe Community College, Legal Assistant Certificate, 2659 Lake Tahoe Boulevard, P.O. Box 14445, South Lake Tahoe, CA 95702

Los Angeles City College, Law Department, 855 North Vermont Avenue, Los Angeles, CA 90029

Los Angeles Southwest College, Legal Assistant Program, 1600 West Imperial Highway, Los Angeles, CA 90047

Merritt College, 12500 Campus Drive, Oakland, CA 94619

Metropolitan Business College, 2390 Pacific College, Long Beach, CA 90806

Metropolitan Technical Institute & Business College, Legal Technician

Program, 1963 North E Street, Suite A, San Bernardino, CA 92405

MTI Western Business College, Legal Assistant Program, 2731 Capital Avenue, Sacramento, CA 95816

Muir Technical Programs, Paralegal Program, 4304 Twain Avenue, San Diego, CA 92120

National Academy for Paralegal Studies, Inc., 8615 Knott Avenue, Suite 11, Buena Park, CA 90620

Orange Coast College, 2701 Fairview Road, Costa Mesa, CA 92626

Pacific Coast College, 118 West Fifth Street, Santa Ana, CA 92701

Pacific College of Legal Careers, Paralegal Studies Program, 580 University Avenue, Sacramento, CA 95825

Pacific Legal Arts College, 1387 Del Norte Road, Camarillo, CA 93010

Pasadena City College, Business Department, 1570 East Colorado Boulevard, Pasadena, CA 91106

Pepperdine University, Legal Studies Program, 24255 Pacific Coast Highway, Malibu, CA 90265-4738

* Rancho Santiago College, Seventeenth at Bristol, Santa Ana, CA 92706

* Rio Hondo College, Paralegal Program, 3600 Workman Mill Road, Whittier, CA 90608

Rutledge College of San Diego, 5620 Kearney Mesa Road, San Diego, CA 92111

Saddleback College, Legal Assistant Program, 28000 Marguerite Parkway, Mission Viejo, CA 92692

* Saint Mary's College, Paralegal Program, P.O. Box 3052, Moraga, CA 94575

San Bernardino Valley College, Legal Administration Program, 701 South Mt. Vernon Avenue, San Bernardino, CA 92403

San Francisco State University, Extended Education–Paralegal Studies, 1600 Holloway Avenue, San Francisco, CA 94132-1789

San Joaquin College of Law, Paralegal Program, 3385 East Shields, Fresno, CA 93726

San Jose State University, Legal Assistant Studies/Cont. Education, One Washington Square, San Jose, CA 95192

Santa Clara University, Institute for Paralegal Education, Lawhouse, Santa Clara, CA 95050

Sawyer College of Business, 6832 Van Nuys Boulevard, Van Nuys, CA 91405

Skyline College, Paralegal Program, 3300 College Drive, San Bruno, CA 94066

Sonoma State University, Attorney Assistant Program, Office of Extended Education, 1801 East Cotati Avenue, Rohnert Park, CA 94928

Unilex College, Paralegal Division, 995 Market Street, San Francisco, CA 94103

* University of California–Extension, Program in Legal Assistantship, P.O. Box AZ, Irvine, CA 92716

University of California–Extension, Certificate in Legal Assistantship, Riverside, CA 92521

University of California–Extension, Program in Legal Assistantship, Santa Barbara, CA 93106

University of California–Extension, Program in Legal Assistantship, Santa Cruz, CA 95064

University of California, Los Angeles–Extension, Attorney Assistant Training Program, 10995 LeConte Avenue, Suite 517, Los Angeles, CA 90024

University of California, San Diego, Legal Assistant Training Program, X-001, La Jolla, CA 92093

University of LaVerne, College of Law, 5445 Balboa Boulevard, Encino, CA 91316

University of LaVerne, 1950 Third Street, LaVerne, CA 91750

University of Northern California, Paralegal School, 816 H Street, Suite 108, Sacramento, CA 95814

* University of San Diego, Lawyer's Assistant Program, Room 318, Serra Hall, Alcala Park, San Diego, CA 92110

University of San Francisco, Paralegal Studies Program, Ignatian Heights, Lone Mountain, San Francisco, CA 94117-1080 (This program was not part of the ABA's list.)

University of Southern California, Paralegal Program, Law Center–University Park, Los Angeles, CA 90089-0071

* University of West Los Angeles, School of Paralegal Studies, 12201 Washington Place, Los Angeles, CA 90066

Watterson College, 336 Rancheros Drive, Suite C, San Marcos, CA 92069

West Valley College, Office of Community Development, 14000 Fruitvale Avenue, Saratoga, CA 95070

Colorado

* Arapahoe Community College, Legal Assistant Program, 5900 South Santa Fe Drive, Littleton, CO 80120

Community College of Denver, Auraria Campus, Service Occupation Div., Room CA-313, 1111 West Colfax, Denver, CO 80204

* Denver Paralegal Institute, General Practice Legal Assistant Program, 1401 19th Street, Denver, CO 80202

Metropolitan State College, Legal Assistant Program, 1006 11th Street, Denver, CO 80204

National Academy for Paralegal Studies, Inc., 950 South Cherry Street, Suite 1000, Denver, CO 80222

Pikes Peak Community College, 5675 South Academy Boulevard, Box 19, Colorado Springs, CO 80906

University of Denver, College of Law, Program of Advanced Professional Development, 200 West 14th Avenue, Denver, CO 80204

University of Southern Colorado, School of Liberal Arts, 2200 Bonforte Boulevard, Pueblo, CO 81001

Connecticut

Connecticut Institute for Paralegal Studies, Inc., 441 Summer Street, Stamford, CT 06901

Fairfield University, North Benson Road, CNS-9, Fairfield, CT 06430

* Hartford College for Women, Legal Assistant Program, The Counseling Center, 50 Elizabeth Street, Hartford, CT 06105

* Manchester Community College, Legal Assistant Program, 60 Bidwell Street, Manchester, CT 06040

* Mattatuck Community College, Legal Assistant Program, 750 Chase Parkway, Waterbury, CT 06708

National Academy for Paralegal Studies, Inc., 339 Main Street, P.O. Box 4102, Yalesville, CT 06492

* Norwalk Community College, Legal Assistant Program, 333 Wilson Avenue, Norwalk, CT 06854

Post College, Legal Assistant Program, 800 Country Club Road, Waterbury, CT 06708

* Quinnipiac College, Legal Studies Department, Mount Carmel Avenue, Hamden, CT 06518

* Sacred Heart University, 5151 Park Avenue, Fairfield, CT 06432

* University of Bridgeport, Law Center/Legal Assistant Program, 303 University Avenue, Bridgeport, CT 06601

University of New Haven, Paralegal Studies, 300 Orange Avenue, West Haven, CT 06516

Delaware

Delaware Technical Community College, Southern Campus, Legal Assistant Technology, Georgetown, DE 19947

National Academy for Paralegal Studies, Inc., 300 Delaware Avenue, 10th Floor, P.O. Box 25046, Wilmington, DE 19801

* University of Delaware, Legal Assistant Education Program, 2800 Pennsylvania Avenue, Wilmington, DE 19806

Wesley College, Paralegal Studies Program, Dover, DE 19901

* Widener University, Institute for Professional Development, 706 Market Street Mall, Law & Education Center, Wilmington, DE 19801

District of Columbia

Antioch School of Law, Paralegal Program, 1624 Crescent Place, NW, Washington, DC 20009

* Georgetown University, Legal Assistant Program, School for Summer Continuing Education, Washington, DC 20057

* George Washington University, Center for Continuing Education & Workshops, 801 22nd Street, NW, Suite T409, Washington, DC 20052

Institute of Law and Aging, Paralegal Training Program, National Law Center, Suite T401, George Washington University, 801 22nd Street, NW, Washington, DC 20052

University of the District of Columbia, 1331 H Street, NW, Washington, DC 20005

Florida

American Institute for Paralegal Studies, Inc., Southeast Regional Office, 5700 St. Augustine Road, Jacksonville, FL 92207

Barry University, Legal Assistant Institute, Ft. Lauderdale, FL 33310

Barry University, Legal Assistant Institute, 11300 Northeast Second Avenue, Miami Shores, FL 33161

Barry University, Legal Assistant Institute, Naples, FL 33941

* Broward Community College, Legal Assistant Program, 3501 Southwest Davie Road, Building 9, Miami, FL 33314

Central Florida Community College, P.O. Box 1388, Ocala, FL 32670

Charron Williams College, Legal Assistant Program, 6289 West Sunrise Boulevard, Ft. Lauderdale, Fl 33313

Edison Community College, P.O. Box 06210, Ft. Myers, FL 33906-6210

Florida Atlantic University, Institute for Legal Assistants, Division of Continuing Education, Boca Raton, FL 33431

Hillsborough Community College, P.O. Box 30030, Tampa, FL 33620

Jones College, Ft. Lauderdale Campus, 6289 West Sunrise Boulevard, Ft. Lauderdale, FL 33313

Jones College, Paralegal Degree & Diploma Programs, Miami Campus, 255 Southwest 8th Street, Miami, FL 33130

Jones College–Lakeland Campus, Paralegal Degree & Diploma Programs, 2620 Kathleen Road, Lakeland, FL 33809

Jones College–South Campus, Paralegal Degree & Diploma Programs, 3428 Beach Boulevard, Jacksonville, FL 32207

Manatee Community College, Legal Assistant Program, P.O. Box 1849, Bradenton, FL 33507

* Miami-Dade Community College, Legal Assistant Program, Mitchell Wolfson New World Center, 300 Northeast 2nd Avenue, Miami, FL 33132

Palm Beach Community College, 4200 Congress Avenue, Lake Worth, FL 33461

Palm Beach Junior College–North, 3160 PGA Boulevard, Palm Beach Gardens, FL 33410

Paralegal Careers, Inc., 1211 North Westshore, Suite 100, Tampa, FL 33607

Pensacola Junior College, Legal Assistant Program, 1000 College Boulevard, Pensacola, FL 32504

St. Petersburg Junior College, Legal Assistant Program, Clearwater Campus, Coachman Road & Drew, Clearwater, FL 33515

St. Petersburg Junior College, Legal Assistant Program, P.O. Box 13489, Division of Business, St. Petersburg, FL 33733

* Santa Fe Community College, Legal Assistant Program, 3000 Northwest 83rd Street, Gainesville, FL 32601-1530

Southern Career Institute, 164 West Royal Palm Road, P.O. Box 2158, Boca Raton, FL 33432

Southern College, 5600 Lake Underhill Road, Orlando, FL 32807

Tampa College, Paralegal Program, 3924 Coconut Palm Drive, Tampa, FL 33619

University of Central Florida, Allied Legal Services Program, P.O. Box 25000, Orlando, FL 32816

University of Miami, Institute for Paralegal Studies, P.O. Box 248005, Coral Gables, FL 33124

University of North Florida, Paralegal Program, P.O. Box 17074, Jacksonville, FL 33245-7074

University of West Florida, Legal Administration Program, Department of Political Science, 11000 University Parkway, Pensacola, FL 32514

Valencia Community College, East Campus, P.O. Box 3028, Orlando, FL 32802

Georgia

Academy for Paralegal Studies, 8493 Campbellton Street, Douglasville, GA 30133   *577-1660*

American Institute for Paralegal Studies, Inc., First Atlanta Tower, Suite 2400, Atlanta, GA 30383

Athens Area Technical Institute, Paralegal Studies Program, U.S. Highway 29 North, Athens, GA 30610

Atlanta Paralegal Institute, 1393 Peachtree Street, NE, Atlanta, GA 30309

Gainesville College, Legal Assistant Program, Mundy Mill Road, Gainesville, GA 30501

Morris Brown College, Legal Assistant Program, 643 Martin Luther King Jr. Drive, Atlanta, GA 30314

* National Center for Paralegal Training, Lawyer's Assistant Program, 3414 Peachtree Road, NE, Suite 528, Atlanta, GA 30326

Hawaii

* Kapiolani Community College, Legal Assistant Program, 620 Pensacola Avenue, Honolulu, HI 96814

Idaho

National Academy for Paralegal Studies, Inc., 2043 East Center, Pocatello, ID 83205

University of Idaho, College of Law, Paralegal Program, Moscow, ID 83840

Illinois

American Institute for Paralegal Studies, Inc., One South 450 Summit Avenue, Suite 230, Oakbrook Terrace, IL 60181

Illinois State University, Legal Studies Program, Schroeder 306, Political Science Department, Normal, IL 61761

179

MacCormac Junior College, 327 South LaSalle Street, Chicago, IL 60604

MacCormac Junior College, 615 North West Avenue, Elmhurst, IL 61761

* Mallinckrodt College, Legal Assistant Program, 1041 Ridge Road, Wilmette, IL 60091

Midstate College, Paralegal Services, 244 Southwest Jefferson, Box 148, Peoria, IL 61602

* Roosevelt University, Lawyer's Assistant Program, 430 South Michigan Avenue, Chicago, IL 60605

* Sangamon State University, Legal Studies Program, Shepherd Road, Springfield, IL 62708

* Southern Illinois University at Carbondale, Paralegal Studies Program, Carbondale, IL 62901

* South Suburban College, Paralegal/ Legal Assistant Program, 15800 South State Street, South Holland, IL 60473

Uptown Learning Center, Legal Assistant Training Program, 1220 West Wilson, Chicago, IL 60640

* William Rainey Harper College, Legal Technology Program, Algonquin & Roselle Roads, Palatine, IL 60067

Indiana
American Institute for Paralegal Studies, Inc., 52582 U.S. 31 North, South Bend, IN 46637

* Ball State University, Legal Assistance & Legal Administration, Muncie, IN 47306

Butler University, Legal Assistant Program, 4600 Sunset, Indianapolis, IN 46208

Indiana Central University, 1400 East Hanna Avenue, Indianapolis, IN 46227

Indiana State University, Conferences & Non-Credit Programs, Alumni Center, Room 240, Terre Haute, IN 47809

Indiana University at South Bend, Paralegal Studies Certificate, 1700 Meshawaka Avenue, South Bend, IN 46634

Lockyear College, Indianapolis Campus, Legal Assistant Program, 1200 Waterway Boulevard, Indianapolis, IN 46202

* University of Evansville, Legal Paraprofessional Program, 1800 Lincoln Avenue, Evansville, IN 47722

* Vincennes University, Paralegal Program, 1002 North 1st Street, Vincennes, IN 47591

Iowa
* Des Moines Area Community College, Urban Campus, Legal Assistant Program, 1100 7th Street, Des Moines, IA 50314

Iowa Lakes Community College, Legal Assistant Program, 300 South 18th Street, Estherville, IA 51334

* Kirkwood Community College, 6301 Kirkwood Boulevard, SW, P.O. Box 2068, Cedar Rapids, IA 52406

Marycrest College, 1607 West 12th Street, Davenport, IA 52804

National Academy for Paralegal Studies, Inc., 627 Frances Building, Sioux City, IA 51101

Kansas
Barton County Community College, Legal Assisting, Great Bend, KS 67530

Hutchinson Community College, Legal Assistant Program, 1300 North Plum, Hutchinson, KS 67501

* Johnson County Community College, Paralegal Program, 12345 College at Quivera, Overland Park, KS 66210

National Academy for Paralegal Studies, Inc., 4121 West 83rd Street, Prairie Village, KS 66208

Washburn University of Topeka, Legal Assistant Program, 17th & College, Topeka, KS 66621

* Wichita State University, Legal Assistant Program, College of Business Administration, Wichita, KS 67208

Kentucky
* Eastern Kentucky University, Paralegal Programs, McCreary 113, Richmond, KY 40475-3122

* Midway College, Paralegal Studies Program, Midway, KY 40347

Morehead State University, College of Arts & Sciences, Paralegal Program, Morehead, KY 40351

National Academy for Paralegal Studies, Inc., 894 Starks Building, 455 South 4th Avenue, Louisville, KY 40202

* Sullivan Junior College of Business, Institute for Paralegal Studies, 3101 Bardstown Road, Louisville, KY 40205

University of Louisville, Paralegal Program, 106 Ford Hall, Political Science Department, Louisville, KY 40292

Louisiana
Institute for Legal Studies, 3501 North Causeway Boulevard, Suite 900, Metairie, LA 70002

Louisiana State University in Shreveport, Paralegal Institute, Division of Continuing Education & Special Programs, Shreveport, LA 71115

Nicholls State University, Legal Assistant Studies, P.O. Box 2089, Thibodaux, LA 70310

*Tulane University, University College, Paralegal Studies Program, 6823 St. Charles Avenue, New Orleans, LA 70118

University of New Orleans, Paralegal Institute, Metropolitan College, 344 Camp Street, Suite 512, New Orleans, LA 70130

University of Southwestern Louisiana, University College, P.O. Box 43370, Lafayette, LA 70504-3370

Maine
Beal College, Paralegal Program, 629 Main Street, Bangor, ME 04401

National Academy for Paralegal Studies, Inc., P.O. Box 1028, Rockland, ME 04841

National Academy for Paralegal Studies, Inc., RFD 3, Box 2470, Waterville, ME 04901

University of Southern Maine, Department of Community Programs, USM Intown Center, 68 High Street, Portland, ME 04101

Maryland
Community College of Baltimore, Paralegal Program, Lombard Street at Market Place, Baltimore, MD 21202

*Dundalk Community College, 7200 Sollers Point Road, Baltimore, MD 21222

Harford Community College, Adult Occupational Education, 401 Thomas Run Road, Bel Air, MD 21014

Montgomery College–Takoma Park Campus, Legal Assistant Program, Takoma Park, MD 20912

National Academy for Paralegal Studies, Inc., 605 Baltimore Avenue, Towson, MD 21204

Prince George's Community College, Paralegal Program, 301 Largo Road, Largo, MD 20772-2199

University of Maryland College Park, University College, College Park Campus, College Park, MD 20742

*Villa Julie College, Paralegal Program, Green Spring Valley Road, Stevenson, MD 21153

Massachusetts
Anna Maria College, Paralegal Program, Paxton, MA 01612

Assumption College, Paralegal Studies, Center for Continuing & Professional Education, 500 Salisbury Street, Worcester, MA 01609

Bay Path College, Legal Assistant Program, 588 Longmeadow Street, Longmeadow, MA 01106

Becker Junior College–Worcester Campus, Paralegal Studies Program, 61 Sever Street, Worcester, MA 01609

*Bentley College, Institute of Paralegal Studies, Beaver & Forest Streets, Waltham, MA 02254

Boston State College, Paralegal Program, 625 Huntington Avenue, Boston, MA 02115

Boston University, Metropolitan College, Legal Assistant Program, 755 Commonwealth Avenue, Boston, MA 02215

*Elms College, Paralegal Institute, Chicopee, MA 01013

Hampshire College, Amherst, MA 01002

Katharine Gibbs School, Legal Assistant Program, 5 Arlington Street, Boston, MA 02116

Middlesex Community College, Paralegal Studies Program, Terrace Hall Avenue, Burlington, MA 01803

Mount Ida College, Paralegal Studies Program, 777 Dedham Street, Newton Centre, MA 02159

National Academy for Paralegal Studies, Inc., P.O. Box 20148, Eudowood, MA 21284

National Academy for Paralegal Studies, Inc., 53 Winter Street, Weymouth, MA 02189

Newbury College, Paralegal Program, 921 Boylston Street, Boston, MA 02115

Northeastern University, Paralegal Program, Center for Continuing Education, 370 Common Street, Dedham, MA 02026

*Northern Essex Community College, Paralegal Studies Program, Elliott Street, Haverhill, MA 01830

North Shore Community College, 3 Essex Street, Beverly, MA 02193

Regis College, Legal Studies Program, 235 Wellesley Street, Weston, MA 02193

Suffolk University, College of Liberal Arts and Sciences, Lawyer's Assistant Certificate, Beacon Hill, Boston, MA 02114-4280

University of Massachusetts at Boston, Center for Legal Education Services, Downtown Center, Boston, MA 02125

Michigan

American Institute for Paralegal Studies, Inc., Southfield Regional Office, Honeywell Center, Suite 225, 17515 West Nine Mile Road, Southfield, MI 48075

Eastern Michigan University, Legal Assistant/Paralegal Program, Ypsilanti, MI 48197

* Ferris State University, Legal Assistant Program, Big Rapids, MI 49307

Grand Valley State University, School of Public Service, College Landing, 467 Mackinac Hall, Allendale, MI 49401

Henry Ford Community College, 5101 Evergreen Road, Dearborn, MI 48128

Henry Ford Community College, 22586 Ann Arbor Trail, Dearborn Heights, MI 48127

* Kellogg Community College, Legal Assistant Program, 450 North Avenue, Battle Creek, MI 49016

Lake Superior State University, A.S. & B.A. Legal Assistant Programs, Social Science Department, Sault Ste. Marie, MI 49783

* Lansing Community College, Legal Assistant Program, Criminal Justice & Law Center, 419 North Capitol Avenue, P.O. Box 40010, Lansing, MI 48901-7210

* Macomb Community College, South Campus, 14500 Twelve Mile Road, Warren, MI 48093

* Madonna College, 36600 Schoolcraft Road, Livonia, MI 48150

* Mercy College of Detroit, Legal Assistant/Legal Administration Program, 8200 West Outer Drive, Detroit, MI 48219

Michigan Christian College, 800 West Avon Road, Rochester, MI 48063

Michigan Paralegal Institute, 65 Cadillac Square, Suite 3200, Detroit, MI 48226

Mott Community College, 1401 East Court Street, Flint, MI 48503

Oakland Community College, Orchard Ridge Campus, 27055 Orchard Lake Road, Farmington Hills, MI 48018

* Oakland University, Diploma Program for Legal Assistants, Division of Continuing Education, Rochester, MI 48063

St. Clair Community College, 323 Erie Street, Port Huron, MI 48060

Minnesota

* Hamline University, Legal Assistant Program, 1536 Hewitt Avenue, St. Paul, MN 55104-1284

* Inver Hills Community College, Legal Assistant Program, 8445 College Trail, Inver Grove Heights, MN 55076

* Minnesota Legal Assistant Institute, 12450 Wayzata Boulevard, Minneapolis, MN 55343

Moorhead State University, Legal Assistant Program, 11th Street South, Moorhead, MN 56560-9980

* North Hennepin Community College, Legal Assistant Program, 7411 85th Avenue North, Minneapolis, MN 55445

* Winona State University, Paralegal Program, Minne Hall, Winona, MN 55987

Mississippi

Hinds Community College, Paralegal Technology Program, Raymond, MS 39154

* Mississippi University for Women, Paralegal Program, Division of Business & Economics, College Street, Columbus, MS 39701

Northwest Mississippi Community College, Legal Assistant Program, 300 North Panola Street, Senatobia, MS 38668

University of Mississippi, Paralegal Studies Program, Universities Center, 1855 Eastover Drive, Suite 101, Jackson, MS 39211

** University of Southern Mississippi, Paralegal Studies, P.O. Box 5108 Southern Station, Hattiesburg, MS 39401

Missouri

* Avila College, Legal Assistant Program, 11901 Wornall Road, Kansas City, MO 64145

Drury Evening College, Continuing Education Division, Legal Assistant Studies, 900 North Benton Avenue, Springfield, MO 65802

Marysville College, 13550 Conway Road, St. Louis, MO 63110

* Missouri Western State College, 4525 Downs Drive, St. Joseph, MO 64507

National Academy for Paralegal Studies, Inc., 11907 Manchester Road, St. Louis, MO 63131

Penn Valley Community College, Legal Technology Program, 3201 Southwest Trafficway, Kansas City, MO 64111

Platt Junior College, Legal Assistant Program, 3131 Frederick Avenue, St. Joseph, MO 64506-2911

Rockhurst College, Paralegal Studies Program, 5225 Troost Avenue, Kansas City, MO 64110

Rutledge College of Springfield, Legal Assistant Program, 625 North Benton, Springfield, MO 65806

St. Louis Community College at Florissant Valley, 3400 Perhall Road, St. Louis, MO 63135

St. Louis Community College at Meramec, 11333 Big Bend, St. Louis, MO 63122

Southeast Missouri State University, 900 Normal, Cape Girardeau, MO 63701

* Webster University, Legal Studies Program, 470 East Lockwood Avenue, St. Louis, MO 63119-3194

William Jewell College, Paralegal Program, Evening Division, Liberty, MO 64068

* William Woods College, Paralegal Studies Program, Fulton, MO 65252

Montana
College of Great Falls, Paralegal Studies, 1301 20th Street South, Great Falls, MT 59405

Missoula Vocational Technical Center, Legal Assisting Cert. Program, 909 South Avenue West, Missoula, MT 59801

Rocky Mountain College, Legal Assistant Program, 1511 Poly Drive, Billings, MT 59102-1796

Nebraska
College of Saint Mary, Paralegal Studies Program, 1901 South 72nd Street, Omaha, NE 68124

Lincoln School of Commerce, Legal Studies Program, 1821 K Street, P.O. Box 82826, Lincoln, NE 68501

Metropolitan Community College, Legal Assistant/Paralegal Program, P.O. Box 3777, Omaha, NE 68103-0777

Nebraska College of Business, Legal Assistant Program, 3636 California Street, Omaha, NE 68131

Nebraska Wesleyan University, Legal Assistant Program, Lincoln, NE 68504

VTI Career Institute of Omaha, Legal Assistant Program, 32nd Avenue & Dodge Streets, Omaha, NE 68131

Nevada
Clark County Community College, Legal Assistant Program, 3200 East Cheyenne Avenue, North Las Vegas, NV 89030

Reno Business College, Wells & Wonder, Reno, NV 89502

New Hampshire
McIntosh College, Legal Assistant Program, 23 Cataract Avenue, Dover, NH 03820

National Academy for Paralegal Studies, Inc., 97 West Merrimack Street, Manchester, NH 03101

Notre Dame College, Legal Assistant Program, 2321 Elm Street, Manchester, NH 03104

* Rivier College, Baccalaureate and Certificate Paralegal Studies, Nashua, NH 03060

University of New Hampshire, Paralegal Studies Program, 24 Rosemary Lane, Durham, NH 03824

New Jersey
American Institute for Paralegal Studies, Inc., 75 South Brookline Drive, Laurel Springs, NJ 08021

Bergen Community College, 400 Paramus Road, Paramus, NJ 07652

Brookdale Community College, 765 Newman Springs Road, Lincroft, NJ 07738

Burlington County College, CA 267, Pemberton–Browns Mills Road, Pemberton, NJ 08068

* Cumberland County College, Legal Technology Program, P.O. Box 517, Vineland, NJ 08360

Fairleigh Dickinson University, Florham-Madison Campus, Paralegal Studies Program, Madison, NJ 07940

First School for Careers, Paralegal Division, 110 Main Avenue, Passaic Park, NJ 07055

Institute of Paralegal Studies, 453 North Wood Avenue, Linden, NJ 07036

Juris-Tech, The Paralegal School, 100 West Prospect, Waldwick, NJ 07463

Law Center for Paralegal Studies, 374 Millburn Avenue, Suite 200, Millburn, NJ 07041

* Mercer County Community College, Legal Assistant Program, P.O. Box B, Trenton, NJ 08690

Middlesex County College, Legal Assistant Program, Business Division, Edison, NJ 08818

* Montclair State College, Department of Legal Studies, Paralegal Studies Program, Upper Montclair, NJ 07043

National Academy for Paralegal Studies, Inc., One Lethbridge Plaza, Suite 23, P.O. Box 835, Mahwah, NJ 07430

Ocean County College, Legal Assistant Technology Program, Toms River, NJ 08753

Plaza School, Garden State Plaza, Route 17 & Route 4, Paramus, NJ 07652

South Jersey Paralegal School, 302 Sherry Way, Cherry Hill, NJ 08034

Taylor Business Institute, 250 Route 28, P.O. Box 6875, Bridgewater, NJ 08807

Upsala College, Paralegal Program, Beck Hall, 203, East Orange, NJ 07019

New Mexico
Navajo Community College, Legal Advocates Training Program, P.O. Box 580, Shiprock, NM 87420

University of Albuquerque, St. Joseph's Place, NW, Albuquerque, NM 87105

New York
* Adelphi University, University College, Center for Career Programs, Lawyer's Assistant Program, Garden City, NY 11530

American Career Schools, Inc., 130 Ontario Street, Albany, NY 12206

American Career Schools, Inc., 1707 Veterans Highway, Central Islip, NY 11722

American News Institute Programs, 110 Central Park Avenue South, Hartsdale, NY 10530

Baruch College, Paralegal Certificate Program, 17 Lexington Avenue, Box 409, New York, NY 10010

* Bronx Community College of the City University of New York, University Avenue & West 181st Street, Bronx, NY 10453

Broome Community College, Paralegal Assistant Program, P.O. Box 1017, Binghamton, NY 13902

Corning Community College, Paralegal Assistant Program, Spencer Hill Road, Corning, NY 14830

* Elizabeth Seton College, Legal Assistant Program, 1061 North Broadway, Yonkers, NY 10701

Erie Community College, City Campus, Paralegal Unit, 121 Ellicott Street, Buffalo, NY 14209

Herkimer County Community College, Paralegal Program, Herkimer, NY 13350

* Hilbert College, Legal Assistant Program, 5200 South Park Avenue, Hamburg, NY 14075

Hunter College of the City University of New York, Paralegal Program, Center for

Lifelong Learning, 695 Park Avenue, New York, NY 10021

International Career Institute, Paralegal Program, 120 West 30th Street, New York, NY 10001

Iona College, Legal Assistant Program, 715 North Avenue, New Rochelle, NY 10801

Junior College of Albany, 140 New Scotland Avenue, Albany, NY 12208

Kingsborough Community College of the City University of New York, Office of Continuing Education, Paralegal Studies Program, Manhattan Beach, NY 11235

* Lehman College of the City University of New York, Paralegal Studies Program, Office of Continuing Education, Bedford Park Boulevard, West, Bronx, NY 10468

* Long Island University, Brooklyn Campus, Paralegal Studies Program, University Plaza–LLC 302, Brooklyn, NY 11201-5372

* Long Island University, C. W. Post Campus, Paralegal Studies Program, Greenvale, NY 11548

Long Island University, Rockland Campus, Route 340, Sparkill, NY 10976

* Manhattanville College, Paralegal Program, Office of Special Programs, Purchase, NY 10577

* Marist College, Paralegal Program, North Road, Poughkeepsie, NY 12601-1381

Marymount Manhattan College, Paralegal Studies Program, 221 East 71st Street, New York, NY 10021

Mercy College, Paralegal Studies Program, Department of Law, Criminal Justice, 555 Broadway, Dobbs Ferry, NY 10522

* Mercy College, White Plains Extension Center, Paralegal Studies Program, White Plains, NY 10601

* Nassau Community College, Paralegal Program, Stewart Avenue, Garden City, NY 11530-6793

National Academy for Paralegal Studies, Inc., P.O. Box 517, Suffern, NY 10901

New School for Social Research, Paralegal Studies, 66 West 12th Street, New York, NY 10011

* New York City Technical College of the City University of New York, 300 Jay Street, Room N-422, Brooklyn, NY 11201-2983

New York Institute of Technology, Paralegal Program, Carleton Avenue, Central Islip, NY 11722

New York Institute of Technology, Paralegal Studies Program, Building

66–Room 131, Carleton Avenue, Central Islip, NY 11722

* New York University, Institute of Paralegal Studies, 11 West 42nd Street, New York, NY 10036

Paralegal Institute, 132 Nassau Street, New York, NY 10038

* Queens College of the City University of New York, Continuing Education Program, Paralegal Studies, Flushing, NY 11367

Rockland Community College, Legal Assistant Program, 145 College Road, Suffern, NY 10901

St. John's University, Legal Assistant Program, Grand Central & Utopia Parkways, Jamaica, NY 11439

Schenectady County Community College, Paralegal Program, 78 Washington Avenue, Schenectady, NY 12305

* Suffolk County Community College–Ammerman Campus, A.A.S. Legal Assistant Program, 533 College Road, Selden, NY 11784

Sullivan County Community College, Paralegal Program, Loch Sheldrake, NY 12759

* Syracuse University College, Legal Assistant Program, 610 East Fayette Street, Syracuse, NY 13244-6020

North Carolina
Appalachian State University, Department of Criminal Justice and Political Science, Boone, NC 28606

* Carteret Community College, Paralegal Technology Program, 3505 Arendell Street, Morehead City, NC 28557-2989

Cecils Junior College of Business, 1567 Patton Avenue, Asheville, NC 28806

Central Carolina Technical Institute, Department of Community Colleges, 1105 Kelly Drive, Sanford, NC 27330

Central Piedmont Community College, Paralegal Technology Program, 1201 Elizabeth Avenue, P.O. Box 35009, Charlotte, NC 28235

Coastal Carolina Community College, Paralegal Technology Program, 444 Western Boulevard, Jacksonville, NC 28540

Davidson County Community College, P.O. Box 1287, Intersection of Old Greensboro, Road & Interstate 40, Lexington, NC 27292

* Fayetteville Technical Community College, Paralegal Technology Program, P.O. Box 5236, Fayetteville, NC 28303

Greensboro College, Applied Arts & Social Sciences, 815 West Market Street, Greensboro, NC 27401-1875

* Meredith College, Legal Assistant Program, 3800 Hillsborough Street, Raleigh, NC 27607-5298

Pitt Technical Institute, Paralegal Program, P.O. Drawer 7007, Greenville, NC 27834

Southwestern Technical Institute, P.O. Box 95, Sylva, NC 28779

North Dakota
National Academy for Paralegal Studies, Inc., 116 North Fourth Street, Bismarck, ND 58502

University of North Dakota, Lake Region, Legal Assistant Program, Devils Lake, ND 58301

Ohio
American Institute for Paralegal Studies, Inc., 2999 East Dublin-Granville Road, Suite 217, Columbus, OH 43229

American Retraining Center, Paralegal Program, 1900 Euclid Avenue, Suite 801, Cleveland, OH 44115

Capital University Law Center, Certified Legal Assistant Program, 665 South High Street, Columbus, OH 43215

Clark Technical College, Box 570, Springfield, OH 45501

* Dyke College, Paralegal Education Programs, 112 Prospect Avenue, Cleveland, OH 44115

Hammel College, 885 East Buchtel, Akron, OH 44305

Muskingum Area Technical College, Paralegal Program, 1555 Newark Road, Zanesville, OH 43701

Paralegal Institute of the Western Reserve Academy, Silver Building, Suite 201, Public Square, Wooster, OH 44691

Sinclair Community College, 444 West Third Street, Dayton, OH 45402

* University of Cincinnati, University College, Legal Assisting Program, Mail Location #207, Cincinnati, OH 45221

* University of Toledo, Legal Assisting Technology, Scott Park Campus, 2801 West Bancroft Street, Toledo, OH 43606

Oklahoma
American Institute for Paralegal Studies, Inc., 530 Northwest 33rd Street, Oklahoma City, OK 73118

Northeastern State University, Paralegal Studies Program, Criminal Justice Department, Tahlequah, OK 74464

Oklahoma Junior College, Legal Assistant/Paralegal Program, 4821

South 72nd East Avenue, Tulsa, OK
74145

Rogers State College, Will Rogers &
College Hill, Claremore, OK 74017-2099

* Rose State College, Legal Assistant
Program/Business Division, 6420
Southeast 15th, Midwest City, OK
73110

* Tulsa Junior College, Business Service
Division, 909 South Boston Avenue,
Tulsa, OK 74119

* University of Oklahoma, Paralegal
Program, CLE Law Center, 300
Timberdell, Room 314, Norman, OK
73019

Oregon
College of Legal Arts, Legal Assistant
Studies Program, University Center
Building, 527 Southwest Hall, Suite
415, Portland, OR 97201

National Academy for Paralegal Studies,
Inc., Barclay Building, Suite 209, 701
Main Street, Oregon City, OR 97045

Oregon State Department of Education,
942 Lancaster Drive, NE, Salem, OR
97310

Portland Community College, Legal
Assistant Program, Department of
Government Service, 12000 Southwest
49th Avenue, Portland, OR 97219

Pennsylvania
Allegheny Community College, 808
Ridge Avenue, Pittsburgh, PA 15212

American Institute for Paralegal Studies,
Inc., Pennsylvania Regional Office,
LeMont Plaza, 609 County Line Road,
Huntingdon Valley, PA 19006

The Career Institute, 1825 JFK
Boulevard, Philadelphia, PA 19103

* Cedar Crest College, Paralegal Studies
Program, 100 College Drive, Allentown,
PA 18104-6169

* Central Pennsylvania Business School,
Division of Legal Studies, College Hill
Road, Summerdale, PA 17093-0309

Community College of Alleghany County
Boyce Campus, 595 Beatty Road,
Monroeville, PA 15146

* Duquesne University, Paralegal
Program, 711 Rockwell Hall, Pittsburgh,
PA 15282

* Gannon University, Lawyer's Assistant
Program, University Square, Erie, PA
16541

Harrisburg Area Community College,
Legal Assistant Program, 3300 Cameron
Street Road, Harrisburg, PA 17110

Indiana University of Pennsylvania,
Paralegal Program, School of Business,
Indiana, PA 15705

King's College, Legal Assistant Program,
Department of Criminal Justice, Wilkes-
Barre, PA 18711

Main Line Paralegal Institute, 100 East
Lancaster, Wayne, PA 19087

* Marywood College, Legal Assistant
Program, Scranton, PA 18509

Northampton County Area Community
College, Legal Assistant Certificate
Program, 3835 Green Pond Road,
Bethlehem, PA 18017

Pennsylvania State University–
Allentown, Continuing Education,
Academic Building, Fogelsville, PA
18051

Pennsylvania State University at
Harrisburg—The Capital College,
Continuing Education, Route 230,
Middletown, PA 17057

Pennsylvania State University, Berks
Campus, Continuing Education,
Tulpehocken Road, RD 5, P.O. Box
2150, Reading, PA 19608

Pennsylvania State University, Delaware
Campus, Continuing Education, 25
Yearsley Mill Road, Media, PA 19063

Pennsylvania State University, Fayette
Campus, Continuing Education, P.O.
Box 519–Route 119N, Uniontown, PA
15401

Pennsylvania State University, Hazleton
Campus, Continuing Education,
Highacres, Hazleton, PA 18201

Pennsylvania State University,
McKeesport Campus, Continuing
Education, University Drive,
McKeesport, PA 15132

Pennsylvania State University, Mont Alto
Campus, Continuing Education, Mont
Alto, PA 17237

Pennsylvania State University, Ogontz
Campus, Continuing Education, 1600
Woodland Road, Abington, PA 19001

Pennsylvania State University,
Shenango Valley Campus, Continuing
Education, 147 Shenango Avenue,
Sharon, PA 16146

Pennsylvania State University, State
College Area, Continuing Education, 109
Grange Building, University Park, PA
16802

Pennsylvania State University, The
Behrend College, Continuing Education,
Station Road, Erie, PA 16563

Pennsylvania State University, The Pittsburgh Center, 337 Fourth Avenue, Pittsburgh, PA 15222

Pennsylvania State University University Park Campus, Continuing Education, 601 Business Administration Building, University Park, PA 16802

Pennsylvania State University, Wilkes-Barre Campus, Continuing Education, Lehman, PA 18627

Pennsylvania State University, Williamsport Area, Continuing Education, 420 Broad Street, Montoursville, PA 17754

Pennsylvania State University, Worthington Scranton Campus, 120 Ridge View Drive, Dunmore, PA 18512

Pennsylvania State University, York Campus, Continuing Education, 1031 Edgecomb Avenue, York, PA 17403

* The Philadelphia Institute, 1926 Arch Street, Philadelphia, PA 19103

* Pierce Junior College, Paralegal Studies Program, 1420 Pine Street, Philadelphia, PA 19103

Robert Morris College, Legal Assistant Certificate Program, Fifth Avenue at Sixth, Pittsburgh, PA 15219

Saint Vincent College, Paralegal Certificate Program, Career Development Center, Latrobe, PA 15650-2690

University of Pennsylvania, Legal Studies Program, 435 Cathedral of Learning, Pittsburgh, PA 15260

* Villanova University, Paralegal Program, Villanova, PA 19085

Western School of Health & Business Careers, 221-25 Fifth Avenue, Pittsburgh, PA 15222

* Widener University, Institute for Professional Development, Room 135, Kapelski Center, Chester, PA 19013

Puerto Rico
Universidad de Ponce, Legal Assistant Program, avenida de Diego 700, Caparra Terrace, PR 00920

Universidad de Ponce, Legal Assistant Program, P.O. Box 648, Ponce, PR 00733

Rhode Island
Roger Williams College, Paralegal Studies, Old Ferry Road, Bristol, RI 02809

Salve Regina College, Legal Assistant Program, Newport, RI 02840

South Carolina
Beaufort Technical College, Paralegal Program, P.O. Box 1288–Ribaut Road, Beaufort, SC 29902

* Greenville Technical College, Paralegal Department, P.O. Box 5616 Station B, Greenville, SC 29606-5616

Horry-Georgetown Technical College, Paralegal Program, P.O. Box 1966–Highway 501 East, Conway, SC 29526

* Midlands Technical College, P.O. Box 2408, Columbia, SC 29202

National Academy for Paralegal Studies, Inc., P.O. Box 3588, Rock Hill, SC 29731

Trident Technical College, P.O. Box 10367, Charleston, SC 29411

Watterson College, Paralegal Studies Program, 1064 Gardner Road, Suite 105, Charleston, SC 29407

South Dakota
National Academy for Paralegal Studies, Inc., 226 North Phillips Avenue, #204, Sioux Falls, SD 57102

Yankton College, Legal Assistant Program, 12th & Douglas, Yankton, SD 57078

Tennessee
Bristol University, Bristol College Drive, Bristol, TN 37620

* Cleveland State Community College, Legal Assistant Program, P.O. Box 3570, Cleveland, TN 37320-3570

Jackson State Community College, Office of Continuing Education, P.O. Box 2467, Jackson, TN 38302-2467

Memphis State University, Department of Business Administration, Memphis, TN 38152

Milligan College, Legal Assistant Program, Milligan College, TN 37682

National Academy for Paralegal Studies, Inc., 5100 Wheelis Drive, Suite 100, Memphis, TN 38117

* Southeastern Paralegal Institute, 2416 21st Avenue, South, Third Floor, Nashville, TN 37212

State Technical Institute at Memphis, Legal Assistant Program, 5983 Macon Cove, Memphis, TN 38134-7693

University of Tennessee, Knoxville, Paralegal Training Program, 608 Stokely Management Center, Knoxville, TN 37996-0565

Texas
Career Institute, 3015 Richmond Avenue, Houston, TX 77098

187

Del Mar College, Legal Assistant Program, Baldwin & Ayers, Corpus Christi, TX 78404

Durham Nixon–Clay Business College, 119 West Eighth Street, P.O. Box 1626, Austin, TX 78767

East Texas State University, Department of Political Science, Commerce, TX 75428

El Centro College, Admissions Office, Main & Lamar, Dallas, TX 75202

El Paso Community College, Legal Assistant Program, P.O. Box 20500, El Paso, TX 79998

Executive Secretarial School, Legal Assistant/Paralegal Program, 4849 Greenville Avenue, Suite 200, Dallas, TX 75206

Grayson County College, Legal Assistant Program, 6101 Grayson Drive, Denison, TX 75020

Houston Community College System, Legal Assistant Program, 4701 Dixon Street, Houston, TX 77007

Lamar University, Continuing Education, P.O. Box 10008, Beaumont, TX 77710

Lee College, 511 South Whiting Street, Baytown, TX 77520-4703

Odessa College, Legal Assistant Program, 201 West University, Odessa, TX 79764

San Antonio College, Legal Assistant Program, 1300 San Pedro Avenue, San Antonio, TX 78284

* Southeastern Paralegal Institute, Legal Assistant Program, 5440 Harvest Hill, Suite 200, Dallas, TX 75230

* Southern Methodist University, Legal Assistant Certificate Program, SMU Box 275, Dallas, TX 75275

* Southwestern Paralegal Institute, Basic Legal Assistant Studies, 2211 Norfolk, Suite 420, Houston, TX 77098-4096

Southwest Texas State University, Lawyer's Assistant Program, Evans Liberal Arts Building, San Marcos, TX 78666

Tarrant County Junior College, Northeast Campus, 828 Harwood Road, Hurst, TX 76054

Texas Para-Legal School–Houston, 608 Fannin, Suite 1903, Houston, TX 77002

Texas Woman's University, Department of History & Government, P.O. Box 23974, Denton, TX 76204

University of Houston–Clear Lake, Legal Studies Program, P.O. Box 20, 2700 Bay Area Boulevard, Houston, TX 77058

University of Texas at Arlington, Paralegal Program, Department of Political Science, Arlington, TX 76019

Video Technical Institute (VTI), Institute for Paralegal Studies, 2505 North Highway 360, Suite 420, Grand Prairie, TX 75053

West Texas State University, Department of History & Political Science, Canyon, TX 79016

Woodland Paralegal Institute, 5 Grograns Park, Suite 200, Woodland, TX 77381

Utah
* Utah Valley Community College, Legal Assistant Program, 1200 South 800 West, Orem, UT 84058

Westminster College of Salt Lake City, 1840 South 1300 East, Salt Lake City, UT 84105

Vermont
Champlain College, P.O. Box 670, Burlington, VT 05402

Woodbury College, Paralegal Studies Program, 659 Elm Street, Montpelier, VT 05602

Virginia
American Institute for Paralegal Studies, Inc., 500 East Main Street, Suite 628, Norfolk, VA 23514

Central Virginia Community College, 3506 Wards Road, Lynchburg, VA 24502

Elizabeth Brant School, Staunton, VA 24401

Ferrum College, Legal Assistant Program, Ferrum, VA 24088

* James Madison University, Department of Political Science, Paralegal Studies Program, Harrisonburg, VA 22807

* J. Sargeant Reynolds Community College, Parham Road Campus, P.O. Box C-32040, Richmond, VA 23261-2040

* Marymount University, Paralegal Studies Program, 2807 North Glebe Road, Arlington, VA 22207-4299

Mountain Empire Community College, Legal Assistant Program, Drawer 700, Big Stone Gap, VA 24219

National Academy for Paralegal Studies, Inc., 1022 Court Street, P.O. Box 1359, Lynchburg, VA 24505

* Northern Virginia Community College, Legal Assisting Program, 3001 North Beauregard, Alexandria, VA 22311

Para-Legal Institute, 7700 Leesburg Pike, Suite 305, Falls Church, VA 22043

Thomas Nelson Community College, Legal Assistant Program, P.O. Box 9407, Hampton, VA 23670

Tidewater Community College, Virginia Beach Campus, Legal Assistant Program, 1700 College Crescent, Virginia Beach, VA 23456

University of Richmond, University College, Evening School, Richmond, VA 23173

* Virginia Intermont College, Paralegal Studies Program, Bristol, VA 24201

Virginia Western Community College, 3095 Colonial Avenue, SW, Roanoke, VA 24038

Washington
American Institute for Paralegal Studies, Inc., 1700 Security Pacific Plaza, 777 108th Avenue, NE, Bellevue, WA 98004

Bellevue Community College, 3000 Landerholm Circle, SE, Bellevue, WA 98009-2037

Central Washington University, Program in Law & Justice, Ellensburg, WA 98926

City University, Legal Studies Programs, 16661 Northup Way, Bellevue, WA 98008

* Edmonds Community College, Legal Assistant Program, 20000 68th Avenue West, Lynnwood, WA 98036

* Highline Community College, Legal Assistant Program, Community College District 9, Midway, WA 98031

Lower Columbia College, Legal Assistant Program, 1600 Maple, Longview, WA 98632

Metropolitan Business College, 2501 Southeast State Highway 160, Port Orchard, WA 98366

National Academy for Paralegal Studies, Inc., P.O. Box 21873, Seattle, WA 98111-3873

Pierce College, Paralegal Studies Program, 9401 Farwest Drive, SW, Tacoma, WA 98498

Spokane Community College, Legal Assistant Program, North 1810 Greene Street, Spokane, WA 99207

University of Washington–Extension, Paralegal Studies Program, 5001 25th Avenue, NE GH-21, Seattle, WA 98195

West Virginia
Fairmont State College, Legal Assistant Program, Division of Social Science, Fairmont, WV 26554

* Marshall University, Community College, Legal Assistant Program, Huntington, WV 25701

National Academy for Paralegal Studies, Inc., 100 Carmel Road, Wheeling, WV 26003

Wisconsin
American Institute for Paralegal Studies, Inc., 710 North Plakington Avenue, Suite 500, Milwaukee, WI 53203

Carthage College, Paralegal Program, 2001 Alford Drive, Kenosha, WI 53140-1994

* Chippewa Valley Technical College, Legal Assistant Program, 620 West Clairmont Avenue, Eau Claire, WI 54701

Concordia College Wisconsin, Paralegal Degree Program, 12800 North Lake Shore Drive, Mequon, WI 53092-9652

* Lakeshore Technical College, Legal Assistant Program, 1290 North Avenue, Cleveland, WI 53015

* Milwaukee Area Technical College, Legal Assistant Program, 700 West State Street, Milwaukee, WI 53233

Wyoming
Casper College, Legal Assistant Program, 125 College Drive, Casper, WY 82601

Bibliography

American Bar Association. *Guidelines for the Approval of Legal Assistant Programs.* Chicago: American Bar Association, 1973.

American Bar Association Commission on Professionalism. ". . . In the Spirit of Public Service: A Blueprint for the Rekindling of Lawyer Professionalism." Chicago: American Bar Association, 1986.

American Bar Association Section of Economics of Law Practice and the Standing Committee on Legal Assistants. *Working with Legal Assistants: A Team Approach for Lawyers and Legal Assistants* vols. 1 and 2. Edited by Paul G. Ulrich and Robert S. Mucklestone. Chicago: American Bar Association, 1980–81.

American Bar Association Special Committee on Legal Assistants. *The Paraprofessional in Medicine, Dentistry and Architecture.* Chicago: American Bar Association, 1971.

American Bar Association Special Committee on Legal Assistants. *The Training and Use of Legal Assistants: A Status Report.* Chicago: American Bar Association, 1974.

American Bar Foundation. *Supplement to the Lawyer Statistical Report: The U.S. Legal Profession in 1985.* Chicago: American Bar Foundation, 1986.

"Arbitration: Fast, Fair and Cheap." *NOLO News* 7, no. 4 (Winter 1987).

Colorado Bar Association. "CBA Legal Assistants Committee Proposed Guidelines for the Utilization of Legal Assistants." *Colorado Lawyer* 15 (February 1986).

Dunn, Karen L. "In Search of Plain English." *Facts & Findings* 14, no. 4 (January 1989).

Durant, W. Clark, III. "Maximizing Access to Justice: A Challenge to the Legal Profession." Speech delivered at the ABA Mid-Winter Meeting, New Orleans, February 12, 1987.

Fellers, James, D. "State of the Legal Profession." *American Bar Association Journal* 61 (September 1975).

Granat, Richard S., and Deborah M. Knight. "A Computer Training Program for Paralegals." *Legal Economics* 14 (March 1988).

Greene, J. Thomas. "Why Is the Section up in Arms over the ABA Report?" *Compleat Lawyer* 4 (Spring 1987).

Harrington, Linda. "Freelancing for Fun and Profit." *Paralegal Reporter* (Fall 1983).

Helmich, Nancy L., and Roger A. Larson. "Legal Assistants in Public Law: Their Role in Attorney General Offices." *Legal Assistants Update* vol. 5. Chicago: American Bar Association, 1986.

Hines, Lyla O. "The National Federation of Paralegal Associations: An Association of Associations." *Paralegal Reporter* (Fall 1988).

Honigsburg, Peter J. *Cluing into Legal Research: A Simple Guide to Finding the Law.* Berkeley: Golden Rain Press, 1979.

Jacobs, Gordon L. "Legal Technology: Present and Future Trends." *Legal Economics* (November/December 1987).

Jacobstein, J. Myron, and Roy M. Mersky. *Legal Research Illustrated.* Mineola, N.Y.: The Foundation Press, Inc., 1977.

Johnson, Beverlee. "Legal Administrator Grows Up." *Legal Administrator* (Summer 1986).

Johnson, Sally. "Alternatives to the Delivery of Legal Services: A Review of HALT Conferences." *Paralegal Reporter* (Summer 1988).

Jones, James W. "The Challenge of Change: Practice of Law in the Year 2000." *Vanderbilt Law Review* 41, no. 4 (May 1988).

Keefe, Kathleen. "State Bar OKs Appearance by Paralegals." *At Issue* (March 1989).

Larson, Roger A. "Certification of Legal Assistants: A Report on an American Bar Association Survey." *Legal Assistants Update* vol. 5. Chicago: American Bar Association, 1986.

Littleton, Arthur D. "ABA Position Paper on Licensure or Certification, and Definition of Legal Assistants." *Legal Assistants Update* vol. 5. Chicago: American Bar Association, 1986.

Martin, Barbara. "Paralegal Profile: Kevin Mann, Legal Technician." *At Issue* (August 1989).

Mattson, Eric. "Legal Scholars Urged to Keep Writing Simple." *Facts & Findings* 15, no. 4 (January 1989).

Moore, Molly. "Communication Skills Needed by Legal Assistants." *Legal Assistants Update* vol. 5. Chicago: American Bar Association, 1986.

"NALA and NFPA State Positions on Issues." *Paralegal Reporter* (Fall 1987).

Options: New Career Paths in Law and Business 2, no. 1. Philadelphia Institute, 1988.

Paralegal Responsibilities. Deerfield, Ill.: National Federation of Paralegal Associations, 1987.

The Paralegal's Guide to U.S. Government Jobs: How to Land a Job in 70 Law-Related Careers. 3rd ed. Washington, D.C.: Federal Reports, Inc., 1988.

"Paralegal Status Sign: Malpractice Insurance." *New York Times* (December 2, 1988).

"Paralegals: The British Invasion." *National Law Journal* (November 16, 1987).

Polsinelli, Joanne. "Future Paralegal Roles." *Paralegal Reporter* (Fall 1988).

"President Nixon Approves Legislation Creating a National Legal Services Corporation." *American Bar Association Journal* 60 (September 1974).

"Report of the Conclave." *Paralegal Reporter* (Spring 1988).

"Report of the Public Protection Committee." *Los Angeles Daily Journal* (August 12, 1988).

Ruse, Peggy, and Joe Whelan. "Results of the NFPA Survey of Non-Traditional Paralegal Responsibilities." *At Issue* (January 1990).

Schaberg, Robert E. *When, Why and How You Should Use a Litigation Support Data Base.* 1988. Photocopy.

Silas, Faye A. "Is Paralegal Certification Worthwhile." *Bar Leader* (July/August 1986).

"Sires' Paralegal Legislation Goes to Governor." *Los Angeles Daily Journal* (September 18, 1987).

U.S. Bureau of Census. "Current Business Reports." *1988 Service Annual Survey.* Washington, D.C.: 1989.

U.S. Bureau of Census. *1987 Census of Service Industries.* Washington, D.C.: 1989.

U.S. Bureau of Census. *Statistical Abstract of the United States 1985.* 105th ed. Washington, D.C.: 1985.

U.S. Bureau of Census. *Statistical Abstract of the United States 1989.* 109th ed. Washington, D.C.: 1989.

U.S. Bureau of Census. *Statistical Abstract of the United States 1987.* 107th ed. Washington, D.C.: 1987.

Wertheim, Lynda F. "Career Paths for Legal Assistants." *Legal Assistants Update* vol. 4. Chicago: American Bar Association, 1984.

Work, Clemens P. "A New Challenge to Doctors and Lawyers." *U.S. News & World Report* (August 23, 1984).

About the Author

After graduating from the University of Hartford in 1974 with a bachelor's degree in psychology, Barbara Bernardo spent the next five years pursuing a career in dance and theater. She began working as a paralegal in 1979 while continuing to pursue her interests in the performing arts.

Barbara has over ten years of experience as a paralegal and legal administrator in law firms and corporations in San Francisco, New York City, and Hartford, Connecticut. She has worked in the areas of securities, corporate law, litigation, antitrust, mergers and acquisitions, environmental law, employee benefits, and microcomputer applications to law.

Barbara currently free-lances as a paralegal and is pursuing a master's degree in business administration while continuing to work as a choreographer in musical theater. She resides in Sonoma County, California, with her husband, David.